Writin

Pleasure

Anthology

By the Bovey Tracey Activities Trust Writing Group

Dedicated to Rosie Curling

© September 2023

ISBN: 9798854979009

Co-Authors

Maria Kinnersley, Sheila Winckles, Doug Dunn,
Rosie Curling, Leighton King, Brenda Heale,
Arnold Sharpe, Ann Weatherall, Trudy Abbott,
Michael Dudley, Audrey Cobbold, Helen Cowell,
John Beech, Peter Debnam, Peter Duxbury

Proof Editors
Jean Newman, Peter Debnam

Writing for Pleasure

Exercise Prompts

INTRODUCTION

The Writing for Pleasure Group is part of the Bovey Tracey Activities Trust (BTAT), an organisation run by volunteers for members within a five mile radius of Bovey Tracey, providing a range of activities both cerebral and physical.

I lead the group which began meeting on the 10th of October 2019. This was the first group that I had led, so it was a case of experimenting as to what worked. The intention was to write for our enjoyment whether it be fiction or fact, memoirs or poetry. We wrote for the pleasure of it.

We were getting into a routine when on the 16th of March 2020 the whole country went into lockdown. Many of the groups in BTAT weren't able to meet at this time. Our group was one of the few that turned to Zoom for our monthly meetings, mainly consisting of reading to each other the results of exercises that I suggested.

A short while after Phoenix Hall (the BTAT meeting place) reopened in August 2021, we were asked to do a presentation of our work during lockdown. So, on Wednesday the 15th of December 2021 we read a selection of pieces from suggested exercises which ranged from a prompt with just the word 'water', to a dialogue exercise to pieces on the theme of Christmas.

1

It was a great success and led to two further presentations in June 2022 and February 2023.

The production of this book is in response to many kind members who have expressed a wish to read what we have written.

My sincere thanks to Doug Dunn who was a driving force in pursuing this project and who has done the work of preparing the manuscript for publishing.

So now, sit back, turn the page and enjoy.

Maria Kinnersley

Group Leader of Writing for Pleasure

PRESENTATION
DECEMBER 2021

Exercise – Write About Water

Water
by Sheila Winckles

I've always wondered why young boys are averse to washing themselves! Playing with water is another matter – splashing it all over themselves and their friends even when fully clothed is a great game!
I remember our son Peter was just such a mischievous child when he was quite young. Having a bath didn't mean using soap to wash himself. It was an excuse to play with boats and splash around.

I decided when he was seven I would take him to the local swimming pool for some swimming lessons. He thought this was wonderful having all that water around himself – and to play in! Thankfully he became a good strong swimmer.

Water
by Doug Dunn

The Moon while so dry
Holds water inside craters
Shaded at the poles

Shooting stars on Earth
Micrometeorites on the Moon
Shake up the water

Asteroid Ceres
The watery dwarf planet
From the dawn of time

Mars once with oceans
Now with water underground
And wet sloping lines

Warm Enceladus
Erupting out to space
Powered by Saturn's tides

Craggy Europa
Covering warm salty seas
Jupiter making life

Dwarf planet Pluto
Together with moon Charon

Hosting ocean life

Water ice Comets
Release gas around the Sun
Form coma and tail

Life giving water
Throughout our universe
Not just here on Earth

It's a poem using the Haiku format of 3 lines of 5
syllables, 7 syllables, 5 syllables

And exactly 100 words!

Water
by Rosie Curling

Water is the product of two gases - extraordinary!

Its many forms include ice; we are overawed by the strength and majesty of glaciers, the beauty of icicles, the suddenness of hailstones. Snowflakes have unique geometric patterns and can build to deadly depths and drifts.

The sea swells and rages then becomes calm and tranquil - furious bubbles in boiling water become steam, replicated in nature as fog and mist.

Every known form of life is water-dependent for growth and survival.

Medieval alchemists searched for the elixir of life; it was probably in a pitcher in front of them.

Dialogue Exercise - "There's something for you in the garage"

Surprise, Surprise
by Maria Kinnersley

"There's something for you in the garage."

"What is it?"

"Why don't you go and see?"

"I remember what happened last time."

"Nothing bad happened, now did it? Well not that I recall anyway."

"Just to remind you because it seems to have slipped your memory; it was my birthday and I was so excited I went running into the garage, straight into the new car you had extravagantly bought me. I was bruised for weeks."

"Well, talk about gratitude. I get no credit for treating you, do I?"

"I don't drive Beryl. We had to get the dealer to take it back. And then there was the pet you gave me - only you let it loose in the garage."

"Oh, you must admit Freddie was lovely"

"I have to say he was a bit of an acquired taste. Not everyone likes tarantulas after all. And you leaving him to wander like that; it wasn't the wisest of moves."

"If you're going to react like that, I'm not going to give you anything else."

"Beryl, love, I do appreciate your gifts. I like surprises and you have given me some great gifts. It's just that, well, recently, they've been a bit off the wall and unexpected."

"Well duh… that's what a surprise is meant to be."

"Just tell me this, where did you find the money for all these surprises?"

"Not money exactly, Bert."

"What then? Out with it - what have you been doing?"

"I haven't been using money, but I did borrow your little blue card. It is so easy to use isn't it?"

"So, I've been paying for my own gifts? And what have I bought now?"

"You'll have to go and see… else it won't be a surprise."

Exercise -Write about a significant event in your life - one that changed its course (or that of your family)

A Life-Changing Event
by Rosie Curling

My grandparents lived in leafy suburbia, a happy, safe, predictable life. The houses were spacious and well-appointed. The gardens large, featuring unusual trees, ornamental ponds, elegant greenhouses, and croquet lawns.

Neighbours were friends, and happily celebrated many family occasions together, and were equally supportive if adversity struck. It was indeed the best of times.

My grandparents' close friends, John and Marjorie Frobisher announced one day that they were going to America for three months to see their son Alan, a chartered accountant enjoying great success in New York.

Many happy parties followed, culminating in a big farewell dinner party at the Golf Club, as everybody wanted to wish them well in their new adventure.

As the Frobisher's got into my grandparents' car to many cries of "Bon Voyage" and "Write to us" and

"Love to Alan", my grandmother said to Marjorie, "I'm really going to miss you, but will look forward to hearing all your news. By the way, I've forgotten the name of the luxury liner you're going on tomorrow?"

"The Titanic," Marjorie replied.

Life Changing Trip
by Doug Dunn

A few years ago I spent my August in Africa. I wanted it to be an experience rather than a holiday so applied to be a volunteer in Malawi at a small elephant reserve. It was my first visit to a continent I had often wondered about and longed to see. Now thinking back on that month of colourful wildlife and wild living, I realise in many ways it was life changing. One change is a sense of appreciation of our pot-hole free roads. Another is I don't need to fetch water or make a fire before every meal.

Chopping and frying up spicy vegetables now takes me back to suppers under the stars with fellow volunteers. We missed cheese and ice cream and looked forward to eating meat once a week.

While I enjoy long evenings, my bedside solar lamp reminds me I turned it off much earlier in Africa after a whole day in the sun. Alarm set for sunrise at 6am. When I hear birds in the morning I think of the tuneful Wood Doves and Bulbuls singing loudly every morning and evening. When I walk in the moors I don't have the excitement of listening and watching out for elephants, warthogs or baboons but I still enjoy meeting ponies and sheep.

Food shopping was different and quite an event. A two hour round trip each week by land rover. En route, I enjoyed keeping a look out for wildlife in the forest. Sometimes we would give lifts to smiling villagers and return with huge sacks of maize powder. Now I appreciate my two-minute walk to the Coop.

I also appreciate conversation. The volunteers I lived with had many stories of adventures with animals. We all had stories to tell of how we got to be living together that summer. Now I appreciate hearing stories of how people got to be living in Devon.

A final life change that came from that trip was becoming interested in volunteering. Now I volunteer for the National Trust at Castle Drogo.

Some people are afraid of visiting Africa. But someone told me the most dangerous thing about travelling there is the bug of wanting to return. Though not possible to return this summer I am planning a trip next spring to visit an old friend I reconnected with who teaches in Tanzania. We have been in regular contact this summer.

Now I'm ready for another life changing experience.

African Elephant

Exercise – Write a Newspaper Report About an Incident That Occurred at the Mare and Foal Sanctuary Charity Shop in Bovey Tracey

STOLEN £55 MILLION PAINTING SAVES BOVEY CHARITY SHOP
by Leighton King

There was excitement and mystery in Bovey Tracey today as people clambered outside the Mare and Foal Sanctuary charity shop window to get a glimpse of the missing painting by Vincent Van Gogh, known as the "Vase with Flowers".

The small painting, measuring 65 x 54 cm, has not been seen since it was stolen in August 2010 from the Mohamed Mahmoud Khalil Museum in Cairo.

Detective Sergeant Maria Kinnersley of the New Scotland Yard's Art and Antiques Squad told the Mid Devon Advertiser "Van Gogh painted 'Vase and Flowers' in 1887, three years before his suicide. The painting has an estimated value of some 50 to 55 million US dollars."

New Scotland Yard are investigating how the painting came to the charity shop in Bovey Tracey. It was wrapped in a bundle of clothing and left on the doorstep during the night. An anonymous Egyptian horse lover has offered to pay the Mare and Foal Sanctuary $50 million US dollars for the painting and intends to see it returned to its place in the Mohamed Mahmoud Khalil Museum in Cairo.

Mare and Foal spokesperson, Doug Dunn, told the Mid Devon Advertiser, "Because of Covid-19, financially we were struggling and facing the prospect of closing some of our shops – this mystery gift could not have happened at a better time and will see the charity through the pandemic."

The Mid Devon Advertiser
Bovey Tracey Edition
Thursday 22 October

Mayhem at the Mare & Foal
by Sheila Winckles

Last Thursday the police were called out to the Mare & Foal charity shop in Bovey Tracey. It seems a young man had rushed into the charity shop and had started pushing the clothes on various rails and shouting in a loud voice,

"I know she brought it in here! I saw her come in earlier when I was driving past."

The shop manager, Mrs Todd, tried to calm him down asking what it was he was looking for. But he only seemed to get more and more agitated and started throwing the clothes, or rather the jackets, all over the floor.

At this point Mrs Todd felt she had to ring for the police. Their arrival quietened the man down and he was persuaded to sit down and explain what his behaviour was all about. He told the police his name was Peter Davis.

It appeared that that morning he had had a row with his mother about tidying his room and getting rid of some of the old jackets which he never wore. He'd left the house feeling very cross and it was on his return home he had seen his mother going into The Mare & Foal with a large bag. Arriving home he immediately went up to his room to see what his mother had taken.

It was then he saw that a dark green jacket had gone missing, and he panicked. This was where he had hidden something in one of the pockets which was very important to him. Hence, his dash down to the Mare & Foal Charity shop.

"Now young man you had better tell us what it is you are looking for and perhaps Mrs Todd will be kind enough to help you find it," said the police sergeant sternly.

"I seem to remember a dark green jacket which I kept out to mend a tear. Yes, here it is behind the counter." And with that, Mrs Todd put the jacket on the counter.

Peter immediately grabbed it and looked in one of the pockets. He breathed a sigh of relief and said, "Thank goodness. It's here," and, looking sheepish he took out an envelope. "It's a cheque for £500 I've won in a competition. I was keeping it secret so that I could buy something special for my parents' Silver Wedding next month."

Everyone clapped and Peter apologised for his behaviour.

"All's well that ends well", said the police sergeant.

Newspaper Report
by Brenda Heale

The police had to be called to the Mare and Foal charity shop in Bovey Tracey last Monday, when an argument which broke out over the purchase of a leopard print dress that the manageress Mrs Greta Green had just put out on the rack for sale, turned physical.

"The two women were fighting over the dress" said Mrs Green. "One slapped the other and she retaliated by kicking out and catching the other one in the shin."

The women involved were Ms Ava White and Ms Eva Black who both live in the town and are next door neighbours.

"At one point, the dress was almost ripped," said Mrs Green who then called the police.

Constable Lydia Brown arrived and tried to calm the situation down.

"Ms White was shouting a great deal and seemed distraught as she thought Ms Black was having an affair with Ms White's partner Mr Joshua Grey" P.C Brown said.

Mrs Green who in her spare time is training to be a counsellor, talked to both women for quite a long time in between serving other customers in the shop.

"After a while" she said, "they calmed down and reached a compromise between themselves."

They decided to pay half each for the dress and share it. One having it for one week and the other for the next week providing it was properly washed in between.

"We might as well share Josh as well as he's really not worth fighting over," Ms White said.

So, Mr Grey will now move from one house to the other on the alternate weeks to the dress.

PC Brown said, "I hope this solution will prove satisfactory."

No further police action was taken.

Bover Breaks out in Bovey
From our roving reporter
Arnold Sharpe

Due to police action Bovey Tracey's Fore Street was closed for two hours on Tuesday afternoon.

The incident started in the Mare & Foal charity shop. Mr. Doug Dunn, a volunteer worker, told me that he was working behind the main shop when he heard the sound of angry voices and breaking glass.

"I hurried to the sales area," Mr. Dunn said. "I saw two older gentlemen shouting at each other, exchanging blows and hitting each other with their walking sticks. They were causing considerable damage. I phoned the police and told them that two men were using sticks as weapons to attack each other. Within a short time, we could hear what seemed to be more than one emergency vehicle approaching. There was a lot of noise."

The shop manager, Mrs Maria Kinnersley told me, "I saw Doug on his phone and hoped that he was calling for help. We tried to calm the two gentlemen down, with little success but after we heard the sirens approaching, the two men hurriedly left the shop. We started to tidy up the mess with the help of a couple of customers. Perhaps fifteen minutes later we heard a commotion outside and four armed police officers in full body armour rushed into the shop and screamed at us to lie on the floor."

A clearly shaken Mrs. Kinnersley continued, "After searching the premises with sniffer dogs, we were allowed to stand up. The officers tried to calm us down. We explained what had occurred in the shop. They asked for descriptions. We told them one man was wearing a black mask the other a blue mask, one had blonde hair the other grey both appeared to be elderly."

In a statement, the Police confirmed that an armed response team had been deployed in Fore Street, Bovey Tracey, and that the street had been closed for two hours. Two local men had been arrested near the scene. They said that the incident was not thought to be terrorist related. Two men had been released on bail pending inquiries.

A resident of Bovey Tracey, who wished to remain anonymous, named the two men in question as Mr Donald Trump and Mr Joe Biden. Both are thought to be in their mid-seventies, both local and known to have a long history of aggravated disagreement.

The resident said that on this occasion their bitter disagreements must have got out of control but might now, at last, be settled in court.

Mrs. Kinnersley told me that both she and Mr. Dunn were still in trauma after the incident but had suffered no physical harm.

An estimated £500 worth of damage had been caused.

It appears that the dispute arose over the purchase of a Moorcroft style flower vase, valued £9.99.

Exercise - It's Saturday Afternoon - You're Not at Home

It's Saturday Afternoon - You're Not at Home
by Brenda Heale

I ring the bell, but you don't open the door. Maybe the bell's not working.

I knock on the door, still no answer. So, I knock louder. You can't be out, can you? You're meant to be shielding from Covid.

I know you can't hear the door if you are out in the back garden, but it's too cold for that and it's starting to drizzle with rain so you wouldn't be out there. The rain's getting worse and the bags of shopping I've got for you seem to be getting heavier by the minute, so I put them down.

I knock loudly again, still no answer. I shout through the letter box, still nothing happening.

My mind's running overtime now. Maybe you're too ill to come to the door or have had a fall and can't get up. Maybe you've got Covid and been rushed to hospital. Who knows? What do I do now? Ring the police? Ring an ambulance? I just don't know. You really should have given me a spare key.

I knock again, still nothing. What am I going to do?

Just on the off chance, I turn the door handle. To my surprise, it opens easily. It wasn't locked. I go in. I hear a flushing sound and you stroll out of the toilet adjusting your clothes and looking very angry. I get a good telling off for being so impatient. Honestly, Auntie, I didn't know a 90-year-old lady would know such bad language!

Picture Exercise – Write a Story about What You See Happening

Breaking News…
by Leighton King

There was a banging on the front door.

"Who is it, Lucy?"

"It's Geoff, from next door."

"Let him in."

Walter was stroking his chin, totally absorbed in studying the latest live trajectory on his laptop.

Geoff was out of breath, "Have you been watching the news? It's like we are preparing for war with China! What's going on?"

Walter didn't look up from the laptop. "Here's the problem. There's a huge piece of Chinese space junk about to make an uncontrolled re-entry back to Earth. NASA have been tracking it for weeks."

"Yeah, I saw that last night on the news, I thought it was supposed to come down in the middle of the Pacific Ocean…?"

Lucy was standing in the doorway reading from her iPhone.

"Here I found something about the Chinese rocket - It says, normally, they can 'steer' a spent rocket to an uninhabited area for re-entry. But apparently, this is different. The spent second stage is tumbling out of control. Wow! It says it is the size of a London bus, weighs some 46,000 pounds and is travelling at 27,000 Km per hour. It goes around the Earth every 90 minutes."

"What do they mean it is 'uncontrolled?'", concern showed in Geoff's face.

Walter didn't take his eyes away from the laptop screen. "I'm looking at the NASA live revised re-entry forecast, they were claiming with 85% confidence - that re-entry would take place along 43 degrees latitude. Now because of the uncontrolled tumbling, they have a revised re-entry trajectory that places the debris re-entry further north. The latest NASA update for re-entry is latitude 51 degrees, 30 minutes, 26 seconds…"

Walter looked like he had seen a ghost. He closed the lid of his laptop and in a sombre voice said, "that's central London."

First Contact
by Maria Kinnersley

Bob and Ray couldn't take their eyes off the screen. With Ray's laptop open on the coffee table in front of them, they viewed the events taking place around the world from the comfort of their suburban bungalow which gave an element of unreality to the proceedings.

"Who'd of thought it?" said Bob, his voice hushed. "First contact with aliens in our lifetime."

Ray was silent. Usually, he would have responded with some inane comment but today, inspiration appeared to have eluded him. The activity on the screen seemed more important than discussion, with the dramatic sight of spaceships that had entered Earth's atmosphere and now hovered over the major cities in America, Africa, Asia and Europe.

"There has been no appearance as yet," gabbled the presenter. "We are awaiting our first sight of these extra-terrestrial travellers. And if you can hear us, we welcome you!"

"Yep," said Bob. "We sure hope you come in peace."

Only Julie was unmoved. She was intent on the screen of her mobile and had other things to think about. As she scrolled through her Facebook page, she had come across a friend request. Who on earth was Erad and why did he want to be my friend, she thought?

Only as she clicked on his image and went into his page, did she realise the connection between the request and the events unfolding. Erad did not look human. A 'wave' emoji appeared on the page.

"Hey guys," she said. "They're friendly."

Picture Prompt
by Ann Weatherall

It was almost 5 pm. Their whole afternoon had been taken up by searching for information on the internet about painters, artists and auctioneers. So far they had found two similar paintings but not by the same artist. Who would have thought that only three days ago their beautiful abstract deer painting was just… well… a painting and didn't really mean much to them. But now just a few months after Charlotte's uncle had passed away, she was shocked to find that she was possibly in possession of a few thousand pounds worth of art that he'd left her in his will.

Charlotte's husband Phil had just been made redundant, and the thoughts of extra money coming into the family was wonderful news. It would help them pay the mortgage, the bills and maybe pay for a short weekend break away somewhere.

Phil's father had come round to their house to help with their online search. It was a challenge as Phil's father was not very good with his laptop. He'd brought it with him but not used it in a long time and the keyboard was thick with dust and it needed charging up before they could even use it. Phil had sold his own laptop last week to pay the electricity bill. Charlotte still had her mobile for staying connected with people and looking for work, and as she was scrolling through a list of artists, a text message arrived. She told Phil that she would have to leave them to it. She had to be elsewhere, she had to meet someone at a pub in town. They didn't look up or acknowledge her.

She left Phil and her Father-in-Law staring at the laptop screen. Neither of them heard her leave. Neither of them saw her with a suitcase, her passport, and the painting.

Exercise – Write a letter to your 14-year-old self

Advice I Would Give to my 14-year-old Self by Brenda Heale

1) Slow down. You've got plenty of time to grow up in and being a grown up is highly overrated anyway.

2) Having long nails, blonde hair and a boyfriend are not the most important things in the world. You will have all of these and more sometime in the future. They all come and go.

3) Pay more attention to school work, even the things you can't see the point in, and revise more for exams.

4) Believe in yourself.

Letter to my 14-year-old Self by Doug Dunn

Dear Dougie,

It must be very strange to receive a letter from your older self! It's something I've been asked to do by my Writing for Enjoyment teacher, 50 years in your future. How are you? I often think about you but have never thought of writing you a letter.

I know writing isn't one of your strengths. You prefer reading about things like stars and planets and nature. You are finding English lessons a bit of a mystery, without the facts and figures found in the sciences. But it does get better. You'll learn to write essays and a whole dissertation and get over your fear of reading aloud. In fact, I'm reading this letter aloud right now in a café to my writing group. I've even shown them a photo of you (bottom right).

I also know life seems tough with the schoolwork and the bullying. I now know it used to happen a lot in boys schools, even by school teachers. Don't worry too much, it will stop quite soon.

Then there's all the mystery around girls. You don't get many chances to meet girls but you will very soon. This summer you are going abroad for the first time – to Spain! And you are going to meet your first girlfriend. I don't remember her name now but in the photo above you are sitting next to her on the beach. She has ginger hair and looks very pretty. You don't look bad yourself with all that long black hair.

A few years ago, I moved to Devon. Remember Torquay was one of your favourite holiday places? I enjoy living on my own but sometimes feel a bit lonely. It reminds me of how I used to feel at your age. Though, recently I spent a week with my new partner after being apart for months. We are going through a huge virus pandemic at the moment. Don't ask! It meant we could only see each other online so it was lovely to finally spend time together.

In a few years you will meet another girlfriend and go out together on weekend dates in Nottingham. Life gets better! You will do well in your exams and go to university. Enjoy your school days even if it feels hard right now. You have so much going on! It makes me realise how lucky I am. I get to do all the things I love; bridge, tennis, table tennis and art with lovely people.

My only regret is losing my memory. So, when you meet your first girlfriend in Spain this summer, please make a point of writing down her name. Then you can tell me when you reply to this letter!

With love from your future self,

Doug

Advice to a Fourteen-year-old
by Leighton King

Dear Fourteen-year-old,

Have a listen to Mark Twain's experiences when he was your age.

34

"When I was a boy of fourteen, my father was so ignorant I could hardly stand to have the old man around. When I got to be twenty-one, I was astonished at just how much he had learned in just seven years."

Read and re-live the adventures of Tom Sawyer and Huckleberry Finn. You will never regret it. Now that you have turned fourteen, the good news is there is new proof that birthdays are good for you. Scientists have found people who have the most birthdays, live the longest. The World is yours. Live well, learn plenty, laugh often, and love much.

XX

Your 14-year-old self.

Exercise – Write a Piece Starting With the Words, 'It was a dark and stormy night'

It was a Dark and Stormy Night
by Trudy Abbott

It was a dark and stormy night, the sound of the thunder gave us such a fright.

The flash of the lightning was quite dramatic, I'm glad I wasn't in the attic.

I know we need rain for the garden, but to be spared this I would wish a pardon.

Sunshine and warmth is my desire; of that you'll find, I'll never tire.

Instead, as I look out, I see fences shaking, and hear the sound of glass breaking.

The wind is howling, and so I am scowling!

What about all the people at sea in this? Some would have thought a cruise would be bliss.

They'll be thinking differently now, especially if they feel sick as a sow!

I think too, of the fishermen; they will have heard the weather forecast.

They would know how best to cope in conditions that leave many without hope.

And still the rain beats down, going on and on; campers with any sense would never have gone.

People on flood plains will be worried; off to safety they should have hurried.

As the wind rushes round about, will there be trees taken out?

There were in the storm of '88, when people realised, it was all too late.

After the storm will come the quiet. There will be peace, and not a riot.

It will be time to assess the damage. Some may not be able to manage.

The insurance companies will be expecting a flood of claims for their inspecting.

No doubt some clients will be disappointed when told their cover is disjointed.

How about some volunteers? They would be seen as 'Little Dears'

With their skills offered freely, and matched with great zeal-ly.

Those who saw it coming were prepared; policies were in order because they cared.

Just like the motto of the Brownies; they were wise, so don't have frown-ies.

Dark and Stormy Night
by Brenda Heale

It was a dark and stormy night when my life changed completely. My father, a quiet and unassuming man, was struck by lightning and died when looking outside for our missing wayward tom cat. It was certainly the most spectacular and interesting thing he had ever done.

My mother, with indecent haste, almost immediately struck up a relationship with an old flame who seemed to appear from nowhere, a swarthy man with a gypsy look about him who owned a travelling circus and was ringmaster there.

Within a matter of weeks the cat, which returned safely within minutes of father's death, was re-homed to an elderly spinster who lived nearby, our house and furniture were sold and we were off to join the circus.

In our new life, school was a very hit and miss affair with occasional weeks in various different places of education. My mother made efforts to teach me and my younger sister in between. We learnt a lot from life if not academically. After some trouble with the local education authorities in one place we stayed at, my mother decided to officially home school us and all formal schooling stopped completely.

We were not lonely as there were several other circus children and I suppose as far as the authorities were concerned with us constantly moving, we, as they say, "slipped through the net," though thankfully not literally in my sister's case as she had always been fond of gymnastics and went on to become a famous trapeze artiste.

Myself, I think, because I missed our old snarly moggie so much and liked all animals, and this being in the times when circuses still had animal acts, I began to be taught the art of lion training by a likeable man who went by the name of Leo Lejenski, though he told me once in an unguarded moment that his birth name was actually Jack Jenkins.

My mother, although she never married the ring master, surprised us both within a year of our new life starting by presenting us with a plump new dark haired baby brother. She named him Storm. Which I thought was very apt when you thought back to the night when our exciting adventures had really began.

Dark and Stormy Night
by Ann Weatherall

It was a dark and stormy night, or so I was led to believe. Actually I hadn't got a clue as to whether it was dark and stormy, bright and sunny, wet, dry, windy, icy. I didn't even know what time, or what day it was.

I remembered it being early on in the year, maybe March, but I was just guessing really. I felt as though I had been locked away in this small, smelly damp room for a lifetime. The light bulb that hung from a frayed wire from the ceiling had been partly covered so that all I could see was the glistening sparkly wet patches on the walls that made it look like a fairy grotto, but it wasn't, it was hell on earth.

I sat, propped up against the wall with my knees pulled up to my chest, my arms wrapped around my legs, trying to make myself as small as I could, not just to keep warm, but to stop the rodents trying to make a meal of my toes.

They would sneak up, silently, and catch you when you were sleeping… Sleeping… that's a laugh, I would catch a few minutes here and there between being on rodent watch, and listening for my kidnappers coming down the creaky wooden steps.

I'd never seen them, they always covered my head with what smelt like a sack that had once contained animal food. It was actually a nice smell, and one that I would use in my imagination to bring me back to real life. It reminded me of the days working on my neighbour's farm land. All the horses and cattle, and chickens, lots and lots of free roaming chickens.

That's where I had been, just before being pushed to the ground, landing heavily on my elbow and taking the skin off to the bone. I rubbed it, it still hurt. I'd wrapped one of my socks around it, trying to keep the cuts clean. How many days would that have been now, 4 or 7? I had no idea. All I knew was that my shouts were being ignored, my banging against an old pipe with my shoe was not bringing anyone to help me.

I wondered where everyone else was, my neighbours Jan and Eddie, their son Frank… we were all working in the barn. But that's all I could remember, we were all together and then… darkness. I hadn't heard their shouts, why hadn't I heard them shout?

The door at the top of the steps creaked open and brought me back to the present day. Hopefully, they were bringing me food and water. If I were lucky I would be given a small container of stinking water and crusts of mouldy bread. Thank goodness it wasn't light enough to see clearly; it did help that I couldn't see what I was eating.

Someone in the shadows grunted something and threw a metal tray across the floor towards me. It hit my leg causing me to flinch. I tried to keep the pain to myself and not scream out, because I didn't want them to see me hiding in the dark. The water had spilled into the tray and I tried to salvage as much of it as I could, but there wasn't much left and it was now full of dirt and probably dead insects too.

The door slammed shut. I breathed and relaxed again.

Then very faintly I heard a voice, like a long-distance whisper. I searched in the silence for where it was coming from, and I located it. I called back and asked them, where are we? What day was it? Why were we here?

They answered... they didn't know, all they could tell me was that it was a dark and stormy night.

On a Dark and Stormy Night
by Maria Kinnersley

It was a dark and stormy night. Although the rain had stopped, the wind still had power. Anita could feel it pulling at her, intent on pushing her over. But she stood there, a solid mass; her feet splayed apart, anchoring her.

She lifted her head and shook it as the wind tangled her hair. She laughed. It felt so good. 'Twas the night to be doing mad things.

They had left the youth club early, bored by the activities on offer. Their excitement tonight was to be found along the seafront. It was nearing high tide and they watched the restless waves coming in like unsettled horses, the odd wave crest visible here and there. Then came the sound of pebbles knocking together as the water drew back. She imagined the god Poseidon breathing in, then out; causing the wave to jump forward in a gush; hitting the sea wall with a slap.

Anita strutted over to a footpath that bordered the beach.

"Come on," she said. "Who's going to face the tunnel of death?"

Her friends gazed at her. Doubt showed on their faces.

"Mum told me not to do this when the waters were like this. It's dangerous," said Bob.

"Mum told me," Anita mimicked, as she imitated her friend's voice.

She laughed. "Go on…I dare you!"

He turned away and she smirked as she saw his face redden.

"I'll meet you at the other end," he mumbled as he walked away.

"Coward," she shouted.

She looked at the other, his face eager but stiff with tension. "Ready?"

He nodded.

Together they watched the movement of the waves. The timing of this was crucial. Then, when the wave broke over the sea wall in a perfect circle, then drained from the footpath, she shouted "Now!"

As one they ran. Anita, as she progressed, kept an eye on the sea swell. She could normally time these wave movements. They had a certain rhythm. But others, better than her had got it wrong in the past, with dire results.

Then she saw it, the next wave was building up. She heard the pebbles rattling. She glanced up and saw Bob at the end, waiting.

"Hurry, Bill," she gasped.

Together they put in a burst of speed and reached the end as the wave struck. Her laugh was triumphant as it soaked her hair. They looked on as the water dragged back from the path and back into the sea. They had beaten it.

"Until the next time," Anita said as she saluted the waves.

It Was a Dark and Stormy Night...?
by Leighton King

Peter Davison shook his head and handed the finished manuscript of Eric Blair's new novel to David Astor. "What do you think David?"

It's a great novel, but I still struggle with the "stormy night" opening line...

It was David Astor's idea for the three of them to meet at his London club.

Membership of the Club was one of the perks he enjoyed as Editor of the London Observer newspaper. Peter Davison had the job of editing Eric Blair's new novel.

The cigar smoke in the London men's club was not helping Eric Blair's breathing and his secret battle with tuberculosis.

"Whisky?"

Eric shook his head. "Not for me, thank you."

"I Don't mind if I do...," Peter Davison said without hesitation.

"Service!" David Astor called out loud enough to snare a passing waiter. "Two whiskies and a jug of water. No ice."

The waiter gave a tacit nod, and without making eye contact he expertly ignored other requests for his attention and continued his uninterrupted journey across the room before disappearing through the swing doors into the kitchen.

Eric had booked a taxi to get him back in time to catch the overnight Pullman service back to Scotland. He yearned to get back outside the club and breathe fresh air if any could be found in a post war London.

Coming to London was a real shock after the complete isolation of "Barnhill." Eric was grateful to David Astor to allow him the use of the farm house cottage on the Scottish Isle of Jura while he was writing what would turn out to be his last novel, at age 46.

I agreed with David, "I also have struggled with the 'stormy night' opening line of the new book," said Peter Davison.

The waiter returned with two whiskeys and a jug of water on a tray. Astor said, "Let's ask an expert member of the public... what do you think for this opening for a novel?, 'It was a dark and stormy night?'"

"Sorry sir, It'll be a cold day in hell - or in the month of April, when the likes of me gets an opportunity to read a book. I don't really have time to think. Every working hour is about paying taxes to the government and putting food on the table. Every work day seems to just get an hour longer. Sometimes I feel like there is no escape. No disrespect sir, you are able to enjoy a whiskey, while there might as well be an extra 13 o'clock chime for us workers."

Blair took the manuscript, drew a fountain pen from an inside coat pocket, unscrewed the cap and with one clean stroke put a blue ink line through, "*It was a dark and stormy night.*"

Above the now deleted introduction Blair wrote a new opening line,

"*It was a bright cold day in April, and the clocks were striking thirteen.*"

Gentlemen, I have to leave now if I am to catch the overnight Pullman back to Scotland. Eric stood and extended his hand and thanked the surprised waiter.

The other two men stood and shook hands and Eric Blair departed for the long return train journey to Scotland.

Peter Davison, said to the waiter, "Do you know who that was? That's the man who wrote about the farm animals... where all the farm animals are equal, and some are just more equal than others..."

We have always known him by his real name, Eric Blair, but you may have heard of him by the pen name of, 'George Orwell.'

Note:

The novel, '1984' became one of the most significant books of the 20th century.

The meaning of George Orwell's iconic opening line continues to be a debated to this day...only a few know the truth.

"*It was a bright cold day in April, and the clocks were striking thirteen*".

It Was a Dark and Stormy Night
by Arnold Sharpe

It was a dark and stormy night. It was getting late and following the latest thunderclap most of the crew were looking out expectantly from the third-floor windows.

The evening had started as normal. Red Watch had reported for duty at the usual time of 1800 hours, the roll call had been taken and Blue Watch dismissed. We would not see them again until 0900 hours the following day.

The evening's duties had been conducted with no snags. With all the routine work and cleaning finished and uninterrupted by any callouts, Red Watch had sat down to supper. The day had been oppressively close and humid.

Looking out of the Mess Room as we ate, the night was getting darker and more threatening. Thunder had been rumbling on and off for some hours with occasional lightning flickering in the hills.

"We could be in for a rough night if it gets closer," said the Sub Officer in charge. This was followed by good-natured backchat.

"Don't be daft" was the call from an older crew member.

"Bring it on" the call from a keen and younger crew member.

The time was after 2200 hours, and the majority of us were relaxing in the club room on the third floor. Some were playing snooker, others playing table tennis, whilst the rest looked on or watched TV. It's a great job being a fireman on stand-down.

The thunder was now closer with the lightning lighting up the skies. Following an exceptionally loud thunderclap, we were looking down on the parade ground and surrounding areas. The town centre, a quarter of a mile away across the railway bridge, was lit up by the latest lightning strike. The rain began to lash down.

"Told you so," the Officer in Charge gloated, "get ready, there'll be trouble out there soon."

It was then that it happened.

The thunder seemed to explode directly overhead, if the building did not actually shake, I'm sure it shuddered. Simultaneously the lightning struck, lighting up the whole area. Before we could take a breath, the lights failed, causing the emergency generator to activate. The whole area was now in darkness.

The thunder struck again even louder, immediately following what seemed like a dozen flashes of lightening, with all the flashes seeming to go to earth in one attack. The precincts of the fire station were surrounded by wrought iron fencing; the lightning was dancing along its length, the rain bouncing down.

Anyone outside and in close proximity must have been scared to death if not in danger of being badly injured. The rain and the storm continued overhead. A spectacle long to be remembered.

"How long," one old lag called out. "I'm taking bets."

As it happened, not long.

Within minutes both our pumping appliances were on the road, horns and lights blaring. It would be over five hours before we were relieved and returned to base, but that's another story or should I say, many stories.

Exercise – A Funny Incident

A Funny Incident
by Ann Weatherall

We were excited about our long weekend away in the Yorkshire Dales countryside. We'd had horrid winter weather, but at last it was sunny and we were on our way. Eight of us, all couples, were going camping to our favourite place.

It was Easter weekend, and the weather was great, so we had brought shorts and vest tops and barbecue food. We had blue sky, sunshine, no rain, a lovely river to swim in and a pub at the end of the lane. The camping field was owned by Jack, a sheep farmer, and his wife Sue. It was rough but we had camped there many times and we were almost part of their family.

Our tent was quite new, we had bought a ridge tent with an outer flysheet cover to it and a separate entrance, our friends were quite jealous of it, theirs didn't have an outer cover.

The field we were allowed to use was on a slope with a flat top, so we would set the tents up on the flat bit and face down the hill towards the river. The toilet was a small outhouse building with a wooden plank with holes in it to sit on, not nice and always full of spiders and moths, but it was better than nothing.

It would be pitch black at night and the drunken walk back from the pub after having a 'lock in' was hilarious.

So many of us ended up in ditches, scratched, bruised, but always happy and pain free until we woke the next day!

On the second night of our Easter break, we had our usual evening at the pub and then walked back to our tents. It was a bit cooler, so we didn't hang about.

At about 1.30am I woke up to a dreadful smell in the tent and cursed my boyfriend for eating too many pickled eggs. He was fast asleep and wasn't aware of what he had done. I fell asleep but woke up again two hours later to his snoring AND horrid smells and pulled the sleeping bag over my head.

At 5.45 I woke up really cold, freezing in fact. He was still asleep and STILL stinking the tent out. I'd had enough and zipped open the inner tent and noticed that the outer zip had not been closed the night before. That's when I saw the snow! About a foot deep, I couldn't believe it, but now realised why I was so cold. I got my jeans, jumper and my boots on and tried to push my way out of the tent, but I got caught on something. I turned my head back to see what I was caught on and that's when I screamed. There was a sheep complete with curly horns, sheltering from the weather between the flysheet and the side of the tent, staring at me and snorting steam! In a state of fear the sheep panicked, trampled on me and shot out of the tent into the snow.

I was bruised and I hurt for weeks, I had hoof marks right across my bottom and my shoulder. But the thing that hurt most was that I'd accused my lovely boyfriend of that dreadful toxic smell and loud snoring, and it wasn't even him!

All in a Day's Work
by Arnold Sharpe

Let's set the scene. Late Summer early 1970's. Gosh, 50 years ago. Have I aged that much?

It's early morning on a dairy farm in the hills above Keighley. The farmer has been milking his herd for the previous hour with no sign of what was about to happen. He released the latest cow to be milked and ushered her out of the milking shed. For no apparent reason the cow bolted and raced across the farm yard and straight towards the midden. For those who don't know what a midden is, it's the area where the farmer stores his cow dung after cleaning the mistal each morning and evening after milking.

It was late August so quite a number of tons had accumulated since he last spread the refuse on his meadows. Up to press I have been reserved in my terminology. During the long hot summer, the dung had formed a hard crust over all but the latest deposits. Avoiding these latest deposits, the cow made it three quarters of the way across the midden before the hard crust gave way leaving the one-ton cow firmly stuck in five feet of farmyard excrement with only its head showing.

That's where my part of the story begins. It was early morning perhaps around 6.30am when the bells went down. One pump was dispatched to the farm. Cow stuck in midden, our only information. It's always interesting turning out to a farm because most farmers have a strong aversion to putting the farm's name at the end of their lane.

Upon arrival, the Leading Fireman in charge realised more manpower would be required if the cow was to be extracted. So the request was sent to Brigade Control to make pumps two for manpower reasons. Whilst waiting for the second pump to arrive work started to release the cow. All animals, cows or horses in particular, can go into shock and quickly die if not cared for when trapped, so one fireman was told to keep the cow calm. This can be done by holding the animals head and whispering sweet nothings into its ear. Believe me it works. Doesn't she have beautiful brown eyes was one remark and this set the mood for the rest of the incident.

Under a clear blue sky, with the temperature rising as the work continued, firemen were stripped to the waste digging away the manure. The second pump had arrived by this time and the plan was to dig under the cow's belly and thread several hosepipes to allow a concerted tug of war to pull the cow clear. Up to our armpits in the proverbial is a good way to describe how we were at that time. See, there are a number of different words that can be used to describe the same thing.

The first effort to pull the cow clear failed miserably even with ten burly firemen straining away. More manure had to be removed. The second attempt was better, and the cow began to slowly move. By this time, we had been working for almost two hours.

Control must have thought that due to the time being taken a senior officer was required to supervise. A senior officer arrived and started to don his fire kit. We were straining and pulling when the Leading Fireman started shouting "she's getting away." On hearing this, the senior officer, who we only vaguely knew, rushed towards us and got to within five yards or so before crashing through the crust and he too was up to his arm pits in cow droppings. His bright clean uniform now utterly ruined.

The farmer was seen scratching his head at the scene he was witnessing. Ten firemen rolling about in hysterics at the plight of the senior officer.

We were to suffer the revenge of that officer for many weeks to come, but it was agreed it was well worth it to see his embarrassment, and the state he was in when we pulled him clear.

You must have thought I had forgotten our cow with the beautiful brown eyes, but no. After extricating our now furious leader, we tackled the cow with renewed energy and out she popped like a cork from a bottle. A vet turned up on the scene and after an examination and a rest in the stalls, she made a full recovery and supplied many more gallons of milk before her time finished.

It makes your day worthwhile when you pull someone or in this case a cow out of the shit.

The Spangled Rooster
by Maria Kinnersley

Back in the late 1970s, I was a newly qualified environmental health officer and still relatively inexperienced. I was in what was called the General Section. One of my roles was the investigation of complaints; anything from odours, drainage problems to noise. This particular blisteringly hot summer day I had gone off in my trusty red Triumph Toledo in response to a vague noise complaint. The address given was that of a cottage in the village of Lower Grumbla.

Having driven through the village twice without realising it, I finally came to a halt outside two cottages that comprised the whole of Lower Grumbla.

For a moment, I wondered whether it was a practical joke thought up by my male colleagues (as they were fond of doing) but decided to visit the left-hand property just to check. After all, there would be no harm done.

A glance confirmed that following rain the night before, the path leading to the property was muddy. I pulled on my wellies, picked up my clipboard with the complaint sheet and opened the gate.

I heard a faint noise and as I turned back, I was confronted by a rooster who stood a few feet away from me with red eyes, his head cocked at me and a mean expression on its face.

Back then, I didn't scare easily. So, I walked forward, waving my clipboard thinking that it would go back the way from which it had appeared.

"Come on now," I said. "Let me through."

But the rooster thought nothing of the difference in our sizes. As I stepped further down the path it flew at me without warning, talons first. I tried again, only to get the same response. I had a watch-bird on my hands!

Now, they tell you not to get annoyed with animals. They don't understand apparently. But this was one majorly angry bird. Any movement I made, it responded to. And I was getting fed up with being flown at. So, the next time it came at me, I kicked out and connected with its chest. It had absolutely no effect. In fact, a rhythm then developed with it flying up at me and me kicking out. It wouldn't stop.

Now I was scared. I did what any sane woman would do. I screamed for help over and over again with the bird really getting into its stride.

Finally, I heard movement and looked over to the right. There on a wall was a small terrier. Seeing the bird, he gave a bark and jumped down. The brave rooster vanished. Then I heard laughter. Looking down I could see why. I had been wearing a black skirt, but from waist to hem, I was covered with the muddy footprints of the bird.

Dragging my dignity with me, I left a note of my visit at the cottage door. The lady I had amused was the one who had made the complaint - of the rooster crowing at first light.

I was then left with the job of explaining to those I met the reason for my original skirt pattern that day.

Exercise - Christmas Thoughts

Father Christmas and his Robin
by Sheila Winckles

It was 7 o'clock on Christmas Eve and the gentle snow was covering the garden. The seven-year-old twins, Jeremy and Peter were dressed in their pyjamas and were staring rapturously out of their bedroom window.

"Oh! look! it's going to be a white Christmas just as it should be!"

"Come along boys it's time you were in your beds. Father Christmas won't come if you are awake!"

"OK mum. Here we go!" and with that, the boys leapt into their beds just as their father came round the door.

"Here you are, boys. I've brought your stockings. Make sure you hang them the right way up for Father Christmas."

And with that, he threw his old football socks - one to each boy so that it landed on their faces saying to them, "Isn't it exciting having Christmas in our new house in Bovey Tracey?"

"Oo yes," the boys exclaimed - Then as twins, they both had the same thought and looking alarmed shouted together:

"But how will Father Christmas know we have moved and don't live in Wales anymore?"

"Well, my darlings," said their mother as she sat down on Jeremy's bed and their father winked at her and left the room,

"Do you remember when we went out into the garden in Chepstow and started pulling up weeds and turning the soil over, there was always a little robin who followed us around?"

"Oh! yes, we remember," both boys said looking puzzled.

"Well, what I didn't tell you was that I had a strong suspicion that that particular robin was a pet of Father Christmas. In fact, all robins are his friends and that is why he gave them red feathers to wear on their chests so that the other birds would know they are important. So, you see my darlings, Father Christmas will have known that we moved to Bovey Tracey last September."

"Oh! thank goodness for robins," said Jeremy. "Hear hear," said Peter sleepily.

"Good night my little men," said their mother as she switched off the light and left the room.

Christmas 2021 or I Woke Up at Christmas by Arnold Sharpe

Father Christmas frowned, sat back in his chair, took off his hat and scratched his head. His bushy white beard bristled as he clenched and unclenched his fists.

There had been a stream of unwanted letters that morning. The first he had opened was from the DOGW (The Department of Global Warming). The letter had warned him that reindeer power could no longer be used after 25th December 2030. The reason given was their emissions of methane gases. He looked out from his grotto and viewed his small herd grazing in a field nearby. Yes, he reflected. Where the snow should now be lying deep and crisp and even, there was no snow at all, just bare land. Even so, could his much beloved herd be such a danger to the planet?

The second and more annoying missive was from the MOD. (The Ministry of Diversity). It had informed him that his work over the last few Christmases had caused complaints in certain circles in particular from The Gay Liberation Front, The Gender Counselling Services and Children Over The Age of Five Should Have a Vote Lobby.

Along with the letter was a list of guidelines that should be followed.

1. He should no longer address children as boys and girls as this could upset gender fluid children. This could lead to trauma amongst those who had yet to make their minds up, especially the three- and four-year-olds.

2. Children should be addressed as young persons with no reference to boy or girl, or he or she. Words that would shortly be outlawed.

3. His red coat with white fur trims should be discontinued as this offended the Anti Blood Sport Lobby. It was suggested a rainbow coat with no trim might be more appropriate.

There was a vague threat that if he refused to comply, the Ministry would take action, and this could put his Christmas business in jeopardy. They also warned him that he may be cancelled. He wondered what that meant. He had screwed up the page and hurled it into the waste paper bin.

The icing on the cake had come with the third letter of the day. It was from his insurance company. It stated that he should no longer bounce young children on his knee as this could lead to claims of sexual interference, deviance and harassment, even many years later.

He sat back in his chair and let out a mighty guffaw which relieved his frustration. For goodness sake,

Christmas was approaching. He continued chuckling with a series of Ho Ho Ho's. Bring it on he thought.

He looked around his workshop only to see empty workbenches where his elves should be working, making Christmas toys. This was due to the Covid 19 pandemic. His seasonal elves were finding it difficult to get work permits. Even though elves had been classified as persons at risk, many of them had failed to take advantage. Permits could not be given to elves without them showing that they had been double jabbed. He had pondered over this dilemma, and it had struck him that there were many out of work gnomes in the area. One problem would be that he would have to offer highly inflated wage incentives to get them off their backsides, off benefits and back to work. That meant even more expense.

Money would be no problem he concluded. Later that day the Fairy Queen was due to visit. She had use of a magic money tree and he was in no doubt she would let him use it.

Christmas was still a few weeks away, and he was confident he could supply all the toys the boys and girls had asked for. Sorry, he thought, young persons of no specific gender.

As for now, it was time to take a break, have a coffee, a mince pie and pull out what little hair he had left.

Letter to Santa
by Brenda Heale

Dear Santa,

I hope you are keeping well and Covid free. I'm sorry to be so negative and Bah Humbug at this festive time of year. Not that anyone wants anything as simple as humbugs now. It's all the latest toy and designer labels and this year we're told it's going to be even more difficult to get the right goods due to delivery problems and lack of lorry drivers.

Although Boris has waived aside restrictions for us travelling, it's difficult, if not impossible to be everywhere at once delivering heavy parcels and being careful to deliver the right gifts to the correct destination. I well remember one incident last year when Great Aunt Bessie was more than a little surprised to get the Ann Summers French Maid's outfit that was meant for Fifi in the house next door. It gave her nephew the fright of his life when he answered the door to her arriving for Christmas lunch decked out in her new outfit! I think he is still having counselling for that. I never did find out what Fifi thought of the nice kit to crochet a cushion cover that she received in the mix-up!!

Then there are the so-called rewards for all my hard work. There are only so many carrots I can eat and even the occasional mince pie or glass of sherry that you don't want is not very exciting to me.

Incidentally Santa, should you really keep drinking so much of the sherry that's left out and still ride the sleigh? Have you done a health and safety course recently? I think not!

Also, I'm tired of having to keep polishing my nose so it's even redder than normal. Once it was something I could play down but now it has to be even brighter and shinier for every journey as it's become such an important feature.

So, all in all, Santa, you must realise that I've become a bit upset by it all and I feel my mental health is suffering. So, this Christmas I will be having a staycation and staying put here at home unless you come up with a plan for better working conditions and a substantial pay rise.

Yours sincerely,

Rudolph Reindeer

PRESENTATION
JUNE 2022

Exercise – Write About Writing

Say Why You Write
by Brenda Heale

"Say why you write," Maria said

My mind went blank

I scratched my head.

But then an idea came to me

I write to set my feelings free

To let my imagination roam

Even when I'm stuck at home.

I write because to me it's fun

And something I have always done.

So even when I can't go out

I find something to smile about.

I prefer to write fiction, but how much of it is fiction? There's a lot of ourselves in everything we write. It's sometimes easier to write things down than it is to talk about them and it's often very therapeutic to write down your thoughts and things that are troubling you. This must be why diary writing has been so popular all through history. Seeing the problem written down often helps you see a solution or just to cope with it and wait to see if the situation changes. Even if it does neither of these, it's a relief to write down how you feel about things.

Normans
by Brenda Heale

Slightly over 30 years ago, I was made redundant from the job I had and through a friend who already worked there was offered a job at Normans.

Most of you won't know what or where I'm talking about but it was a cut-price warehouse supermarket located at Trago Mills where the Co-op is now.

It sold some inexpensive foreign brands and I suppose if better managed could have been the forerunner for the giant that is Lidl.

I'd done shop work before but only in a little shop where you put the prices into the till manually so the bar code scanner was a new thing to me.

My so-called training consisted of having a member of staff stand beside me for the first 10 minutes as I worked and after that, I was on my own.

After a couple of days working there, I could still hear the beep of the scanner in my head as I fell asleep at night. The till had a will of its own. Some items just wouldn't scan and you had to hold them up and shout into the speaker to get someone to look up the price. Believe me, when you are holding up and shouting out Super Plus Tampax- no price, it's embarrassing for you and the customer. Changing the till roll was like going on the Krypton Factor and the ever-lengthening queue waiting to be served did nothing to help.

 Being close to 40 I was older than most of the staff and spent some early mornings with young girls on tills nearby telling each other in great detail about their experiences the night before. This involved a degree of shouting as the shop was quite noisy but no intimate detail was spared. A Jackie Collins novel would have seemed tame in comparison and they kept serving customers all the time too. Wonderful multitasking I thought.

There were always various (usually illicit) staff romances going on in the store too. So it was best to knock loudly on the office door before entering.

Sundays were the most stressful day as the shop seemed full of bickering parents who obviously didn't want to be there and free-range children running about screaming or, if quiet, trying to steal the sweets that were in those days set out temptingly close to the tills.

Tea breaks and often dinner breaks tended to get forgotten if you didn't remind the office staff, but I got used to it all remarkably quickly and can look back on it now as an interesting experience.

At least it's taught me to be more patient and appreciate the person on the till especially with so many shops going over to mainly self-service tills now. I think it's nice to still see a real person there.

Writing about writing
by Doug Dunn

I heard on the radio that people in the Arab world found no use in writing before AD 200. Communication was mainly oral through storytelling, myths and legends. Even the Koran, written much later was mainly used for recital rather than private reading.

I tried to imagine a world without writing. How often in a typical day would I need to read or write?

That day when I was listening to the radio I decided to visit a new place; Budleigh Salterton. I wouldn't have found the drive so easy without writing the name into Google maps and reading the directions on my phone. Even the car dashboard required reading my speed. As I approached the town I appreciated finding a car park with a sign saying 'free parking', unheard of around Bovey! then another sign indicating the way 'to the seafront' and another for 'fish & chips' making my walk all the more pleasant.

Another pleasure was sitting on the beach drinking coffee and reading a book entitled 'Brief Answers to the Big Questions' by Stephen Hawkins. Through reading his book I was able to glimpse his extraordinary understanding of the universe. Sadly he died in 2018 after the book was published, but through reading, we can still hear his ideas about the future of science and mankind.

Later that day I confirmed a dental appointment by replying to a text message. I wrote the word 'yes.' So much quicker than calling them up. Then, that evening I played bridge in Teignmouth. Although I didn't need to write anything, I did have to read the cards and use a bidding box containing instructions such as '1 heart' or 'pass'. In the old days, bridge players used to speak the bids but now they are written down on cards. 'See you in 2 weeks Bill' I said to my bridge partner after our game, but we both knew it would be written in our calendars.

When I returned home I turned on the TV and read through the film titles on Netflix. There were several films 'currently trending' many of which needed subtitles.

For better or worse, my day would have been quite different in a world without reading or writing. They are both skills we take for granted but which add so much to our daily lives.

Exercise – Write a Memoir

Drive from San Francisco
by Doug Dunn

This memoir is about emotions. While I tend to forget things I've done, what sticks is how I felt.

It's July 8th, 2019. I'm at Manchester airport waiting to board a flight for San Francisco. I feel annoyed as I hear an announcement that my flight will be delayed by three hours.

I decide to buy some lunch and hopefully speak to other passengers. With this delay, how could I keep to my travel plans; pick up the hire car, drive to Airbnb near Yosemite Park, and next day take highway 385 to Lake Tahoe? It seemed simple enough when I was in Devon. But now I'm now told it's a crazy plan by a fellow passenger from the Bay Area. Trusting he knows a bit more than me about California, I decide to cancel my overnight reservation and follow his suggestion to drive via Sacramento instead.

Feeling happier I speak to another passenger I met earlier in the lunch queue. She loves Lake Tahoe and says I'll have a wonderful time, and whatever I do, I must visit Fallen Leaf Lake on the way.

After a restful flight, we land in San Francisco. I pick up my car and drive slowly around quiet roads to get used to driving automatic and on the right side of the road. I check the route out of the city and note down the highway numbers. It is dark but after half an hour of driving, I start to relax.

Several hours later I start thinking about where to stop overnight and see a motor lodge advertising free breakfast. I feel happy to have found a place to sleep after a very long day.

In the morning I wake to a beautiful blue sun-filled sky, and I am excited about driving to Lake Tahoe. I enjoy my pancakes and maple syrup and keep some cakes and fruit to eat for lunch. With coffee to go, I drive off in search of a gas station.

Having worked out how to open my petrol cap I park by the petrol pump, but how do I get the petrol into the tank? Feeling embarrassed I walk to the station shop and find out that over there you pay for the fuel before filling up.

Back on the highway, I actually start to enjoy my vacation. After a few hours, I notice the altitude rising. According to Google Maps, I should be approaching the lake. Then round the next bend, I see Lake Tahoe; a wide expanse of blue with white and brown snow-capped mountains on the horizon. I'm happy to have made it there. This amazing place will be my home for the next 5 days.

A few miles later, I take a detour to stop for lunch at Fallen Leaf Lake. It really is a must-visit place with clear water, bird life and wonderful views of the mountains.

Lake Tahoe, USA

The drive around Lake Tahoe was also beautiful. I soon arrived at my holiday lodge where I checked in and met the participants on the course I was attending. It felt lovely to be talking to people after a day of driving.

Part of the course was to take part in activities such as kayaking, zip-lining and flying in a light aircraft.

What an amazing week!

Why I Have Failed to Become a Writer!
by Sheila Winckles

When I was young and had learned to read, I joined the local library and from then on I became a constant reader. It fascinated me that there were people who used their imagination to make up stories which then became published, and others would pay money to read them. A form of escapism and I would like to be one of them.

This dream lasted until we moved to Devon and our children had started their own careers and living away from home. I needed an occupation, so I became an Open University student and after three years received my Bachelor of Arts Degree.

Now, I thought, perhaps I'll write a book! But first I'll apply to The Writers Bureau and learn a few tips. I spent several months writing stories, having them read by experts and being sent advice on improvements. All very helpful.

But then I got involved with Church Recording which meant that instead of writing stories from my imagination I was writing the factual history of the ancient churches in our local area. I had a team under me and, working in pairs, we each took a certain section in the church to photograph and research the history.

There was woodwork, stained glass, memorials, etc. etc. Once a church was finished then a Church Guide was made up by me as the leader which went to the C of E authorities in London together with a copy for the church. I also had the pleasure of writing the handbook guide for visitors to Bovey Tracey Parish Church. In all, I led a team recording six churches in and around Bovey Tracey and Newton Abbot. It was very interesting discovering past history which had been unknown at that time.

And so then I thought I would write my book! I've written the outline which, of course, includes a group of Church Recorders. But this is as far as I have got!!!!!

Some of the Things I Couldn't Do Without by Sheila Winckles

It's difficult to choose between the many items which I couldn't do without. Having to cope with the Covid problems over the last two years, something I've needed to get me through the day is working on two of the Times newspaper crosswords. They have kept me quiet each morning when I have my coffee break. (For which David is more than thankful!!!).

However, although I feel I couldn't do without my crosswords, there are some days when the answers to some of the clues won't come and I sit feeling frustrated and annoyed. I'm wasting time when I could be doing something useful.

One solution to this I've discovered is to go away and forget the crossword. Then, low and behold, when I next think of the clue, it comes to me easily. I feel a fool for not thinking of it in the first place.

I laugh to myself then and think that whoever thought of calling these puzzles 'Crosswords' knew exactly the effect they could have on people such as myself when the answers to the clues escape them.

Something else I couldn't do without is having a book to read – especially when I go to bed. Reading a few chapters for me is a wonderful tonic for a good night's sleep. I belong to a Ladies' book Club and taking it in turns to suggest a book to read means we always have a good selection at our disposal.

Writing About Writing
by Michael Dudley

Foreword

I believe that the human species is the most highly advanced, highly sophisticated biological, and technological being, displaying extraordinary creative potential.

Consider the process involved in creating vocal noises like grunts, and squeaks, and then making them loud or soft. Now, eventually, attach meaning to each separate sound, such that another of the species can understand that meaning.

Connect these noises to create even more complex sounds with meanings until eventually a language is created. But don't stop there. Repeat this process several hundred times, tribe by tribe.

Now, invent a tool to leave a mark on a cave wall, on papyrus, on paper.

Let mark 1 sound like… and mean…

Let mark 2 sound like… and mean… etc.

Can this be how writing was created?

The Writing Process - The Blank Page

Most writers and artists start with a blank (either paper or a block of wood, an untouched palate). I almost always sit looking at 'the blank' for the first day after I intend to start writing (sometimes this occurs when I intend to play my violin!).

But the blank page attracts me rather than scares me, for I see the page is filled with possibilities, like a block of wood waiting to be carved, to reveal its hidden shape.

So, I allow possibilities either to get discarded or show themselves and be used in the writing theme which has now just been set.

Once the first sentence is written, the 'blank page' energy in me is charged and off we go, seconded usually by a musical arrangement!! Yes, I sing to myself.

A Three-Year-Old's Experience
by Michael Dudley

Imagine the strange undulating cat-like wailing of fire sirens in the darkened evening sky, accompanied by the droning throb of aircraft engines overhead and the weird beams of light piercing upwards into the darkness.

Feel the unease emanating from our parents as they dressed us, my sister and me, in warm heavy clothing with an awful mask covering our faces.

They prepared to carry us down to the "construction" our father had built at the bottom of the garden (later known as the air raid shelter).

We sat inside watching our parents and mimicked their reactions, not realising that we were learning how to feel fear and express hope.

"It's Coventry on fire," our father had uttered into our silence, words not forgotten to this day, some eighty years later. "But we're safe. They're going to miss us."

Coventry on Fire, 1941

Writing
by Arnold Sharpe

Writing is an alternative to verbal and visual communication. It can be both more personal and less personal at the same time. Take for example an insult. When visual or verbal, it can be shaken off in moments, but when put into words on a sheet of paper it can last a lifetime. This is only one example of the power of writing. Both fiction and nonfiction writing are powerful tools;

The gift of a storyteller to put their story onto paper and keep the reader enthralled and wanting to read more is a gift indeed.

The putting of information into textbooks or other types of books is the main way of passing information from generation to generation. In future, this may be stored in other ways than on paper, even in ways as yet not thought of. Yet in all cases, that information will have to be translated from some form of writing.

I have no ambitions to write fiction except in very short formats. I admire greatly the breadth of knowledge and research that goes into the writing of a novel. I admire more the author's genius in thinking up the many and varied narratives that make their heroes and heroines both believable and vulnerable. The way an author can transport the reader into locations far and wide, almost feeling the cold or the heat, even experiencing noise, sights and smells as well as predicaments alongside the author's main characters.

The sheer hard work that goes into the writing of good fiction is beyond me.

I have said that I have no ambitions in the direction of fiction writing. Couple that with my belief that I don't have the required ability and you may see where I am coming from.

Writing is a great exercise. All I need to find is the correct niche to test what ability I have.

It helps to be part of such a welcoming group like this. Perhaps I'll find a niche for myself along the way.

The First of Many
by Arnold Sharpe

The 2nd of February 1967, a Monday morning 8.30 am, there I stood, outside Keighley fire station, 30 minutes early, full of anticipation, tempered with a dash of trepidation. It was my first day as a member of The West Riding of Yorkshire County Fire Service.

Many friends and family thought I was crazy to join the Fire Service. Why? Well, that's another story. I was leaving a skilled job earning £25/30 per week and taking a job on less than £15 per fifty-six-hour week.

Standing there, for the first time, I thought, perhaps they may be right.

I entered the foyer and waited. A fireman noticed me and inquired what I wanted. I told him it was my first day and I was reporting for duty. I gave him the letter with the instructions that I had received.

He looked me up and down and disappeared. An officer appeared and I repeated what I had already said. He looked at the sheet of paper in his hand, he also looked me up and down and also disappeared.

Ages seemed to pass but probably only a few minutes before the officer reappeared. He frowned and told me they had no information regarding me.

"Are you sure you're at the correct fire station?" he asked.

"I'm not sure," I said, "but that's what it says on the letter."

He glared at me, turned around and left me there wondering what I had let myself in for.

Moments later, I was led into the mess where firemen of the night watch were finishing their breakfasts. Then started the banter that I was to grow to know and cherish.

In those days most of the service was made up of ex-servicemen, especially the Officers. If you couldn't stand your corner, you could be in for a hard time. After working in an engineering black shop, I'd heard most of it before and felt at home.

I did not know it at the time, but Keighley was Divisional Headquarters and controlled fourteen satellite stations mostly in The Yorkshire Dales.

Shortly after 9 pm, I was taken into the Divisional Commanders' office. He brightened my day by saying he was surprised to see me. I shouldn't have been posted to Keighley until after my three-month training course which was not due to start until March.

"Anyway, now that you are here," he told me, "keep your nose clean, do what you're told and don't get in the way."

Dismissed. Yes sir no sir three bags full sir.

I was then taken to Brigade Headquarters and issued with all my new uniforms etc. Back at Keighley, I was given a locker to stow away my new possessions. I was told to come back in the morning, in uniform and we'll try to find something for you to do, oh and by the way, welcome! So started my never to be regretted life in the fire service.

Arnold Sharpe

Tomahawk Accident Kills Student Pilot and Instructor
by Leighton King

Driving back from a meeting, I heard on the local radio news that an airplane had crash-landed in a farmer's field near Oxford.

As each half-hour passed, more facts emerged from the news reports. The 'crash landing' involved a student pilot and an instructor.

As a student pilot myself at the Oxford CSE Flight School, I was keen to know more.

It wasn't unusual to practice emergency landings with the engine at idle, or sometimes off. Perhaps they just got too low, I thought, or they couldn't get the engine restarted and had to make a real emergency landing.

Then there was worse news. This was not a 'landing' accident but, from the way a witness described the event, "The aircraft just dropped out of the sky and hit the ground". It began to look like a failure to recover from a spin.

Then came the worst news of all. There were two fatalities. The news was almost impossible to accept. One of the fatalities was my very good friend - my flight instructor.

The PA-38, "Tomahawk" is one of the Oxford-based, CSE pilot training school's two-seat training aircraft.

Why do I write?
by Ann Weatherall

Well, I can honestly tell you that I write because I can. I'm very fortunate to have learnt to read and write at primary school over 60 years ago. And I am so pleased that I had this opportunity which many young people in poorer countries didn't have.

I started school late, and most of my friends had almost 5 months of learning ahead of me. This made things difficult for me and I trailed behind the other children for a while. But I caught up quickly and I was soon reading Ladybird books and then moving up to Enid Blyton stories and Rupert.

But then I had a problem in my early teens, I would get my words mixed up and what was in my head came out differently when I wrote it down on paper. My teacher thought I was Dyslexic, but tests didn't show any problems, so nothing more was said about it and I was left to sort it out myself. I avoided having to write if I could, but, as I got older and school essays had to be written for exam results, I struggled again.

I managed to get a teacher who took the time to help me, and I am so pleased that she persevered with me.

My writing and connection to my brain improved and soon it wasn't a problem anymore, it just took me a little longer than other children in my class, but at least what I was writing now made sense.

As I got older, writing became a big part of my life. I found in my late 20s that I was having problems speaking out. I could read out loud from something written down on paper, but I couldn't do it without. My words would jumble up and I would say the most ridiculous things! So my way of overcoming this was to write down what I wanted to say and then read them out. This helped me so much.

So my love of writing had started. I could express myself in my own words whenever I wanted to. I would write down poems, stories, my feelings, my anger, my happiness… just anything that came to me. Writing is a very powerful way of telling your own story in your own words.

My Favourite Place in Devon
by Ann Weatherall

After walking along the gravel track for about 35 minutes my feet were now telling me a different story, that it had been much longer, and my poor stomach was crying out for food. My water bottle was almost empty and the dust from the very well-walked path was sticking in my throat and tasted powdery.

Surely, I was near the end of the walk by now; if it was going to be much further then I must have been told wrongly when I'd asked for directions at the beginning of my walk.

This was how I found my favourite place in Devon, by taking a wrong turn and being too stubborn to turn around and go back to the original path. I'd kept walking, hoping I would see a landmark that I recognised, but I didn't. This was new territory to me, but then as I turned a corner by an old stone fence post the view in front of me was absolutely stunning.

I then knew where I was, but I had reached it from a different direction. And what a fabulous view it was!

As I stood still in the sunshine, breathing deeply, I could feel my heart beating… thump, thump, thump, thump. Then as if someone had turned the sound up I could hear the birds and the sound of waves caressing the pebbled shore, the seagulls screaming and the hum of bees.

I walked a little further and sat down on the soft grass on top of the cliff edge overlooking a small cove. I took my shoes off and I touched the ground with both my hands and bare feet. I could feel the vibrations of the sea crashing into the caves below.

I felt grounded and connected with the world.

This newfound little piece of heaven became my favourite place in Devon.

A Well- Remembered Devon Place – Bellamarsh
by Brenda Heale

I was born and lived the first 15 years of my life at Bellamarsh Mill House. Bellamarsh was originally called Bellamarsh Barton and was a hamlet of 2 cottages, a large farm, a working mill and our house which we ran as a smallholding all year round and also did bed and breakfast and evening meal (if required) during the summer months. It's situated about 2 miles from Chudleigh.

It was all owned by Lord Clifford. My uncle Elford was the miller and I often looked around the mill when all the machinery was in action and found it fascinating.

There was a millpond with the mill wheel where we swam in the summer months. It was only later I found out the significance of the building as it was where the 1795 bread riots started.

The miller at that time was called James Ball. The price of wheat had rocketed, and it was the general opinion of the labourers that supplies were being held back to increase profits, though we don't know if Mr Ball was guilty of that.

Very bad weather had affected the growth of other food staples – potatoes, greens, turnips and swedes and the plight of the labourers was desperate. Their wages had hardly increased at all, going from just 1s 2d per day in 1700 to 1s 4d per day in 1790 but the price of food had soared.

Thomas Campion was 30 years old with elderly parents to support. He was persuaded by others to lead the riots and they broke into the mill and caused damage to the machinery.

Thomas and 4 others were taken into custody. The other 4 were finally released but it was decided that Thomas would be hanged as an example to other would-be troublemakers.

The hanging took place at Gappah Brake and was the last public execution in this county.

My brother said on several occasions he woke up and could hear the mob walking Thomas Campion up the hill to his place of execution. So, his spirit did not rest.

A very sad thing about all this is that although now the mill would be classed as a listed building and a place of historic interest, during the 1960s, when only new things were generally thought to be of any value, the mill and the 2 cottages were all demolished.

One of Our Favourite Places in Devon
by Sheila Winckles

In the '90s when our six grandchildren were all youngsters, they would spend much of the summer holidays together with David and me here in Devon.

It was great fun being all together and one of our favourite places on a lovely sunny day was to spend it at Blackpool Sands. This would mean we travelled in two or three cars packed with mountains of food and drinks, buckets and spades as well as folding chairs, rugs and towels. What a performance!

But we went off singing and the children bragging about how much swimming they were going to do and the rocks they were going to climb.

Blackpool Sands was a popular place for families such as ours and the amenities were just right - a good car park and the kiosk for ice cream which could run out if you didn't buy it early enough!

As you can imagine, David and I were able to relax whilst all the children had to be carefully watched by their parents when they went rushing off to go in the sea or climb on the rocks.

But these days were wonderful memories and we all enjoyed being together so much.

As you can imagine, putting the grandchildren to bed meant they became quiet very quickly after such an active day.

Now all our grandchildren are young adults leading their own lives but thankfully they come to stay with us as often as they can. We talk about all the happy times we had together when they were young and all the exciting places we have visited in lovely Devon.

Blackpool Sands

A Favourite Place in Devon
by Arnold Sharpe

Saddle Tor

My favourite place is not a place at all. It's an area. Climb Saddle Tor, look towards Widecombe, and turn right. Just follow the paths,

"What paths?" you may ask. "There are no paths." In that respect you are correct.

No paths but numerous animal tracks. Just follow your nose and see where it takes you. The many rocky outcrops can have one's imagination doing overtime.

Walk from outcrop to outcrop; some of the paths are well-trodden. Others not.

No matter the season, no matter the time of day, what you see changes by the hour. The colours can be bright, they can be sombre. But whenever they are seen, they calm even the most troubled of minds. The heathers, the gorse and the many wildflowers and plants are a joy to see and change season to season. Look around you and the views vary in every direction. Far and near the landscapes are a sight to behold.

All this and we haven't mentioned the wildlife. The ponies, the cattle and the sheep roam almost freely from one area of pasture to the next. Theirs are the paths you are now treading.

Then there are the animals rarely seen but nevertheless, live their lives here. The moor is a quiet place if you are deaf, but full of noise if you wish to listen.

As with the flora, the fauna changes. The sound of the larks chattering to lead you away from their nest sites. The cuckoo heard but rarely seen. The haunting sound of the curlew. The wheatear and the many other species that only the knowledgeable can name.

The sights and sounds can be shared in the company of others but if one wishes to experience full serenity, sit alone, listen and enjoy the tranquillity. Your only companion, maybe, your faithful dog sat at your feet.

My Jack Frost

My Favourite Place in Devon
by Doug Dunn

My favourite place to visit in Devon is Castle Drogo. What makes this National Trust property stand out? I like the other properties I have visited, but this one is special for me because I volunteered there for a year as a room guide.

Since it reopened after Covid, I have been unsure whether to return to volunteering. Had I got out of the habit of working there each Tuesday or had I just lost interest?

Then recently, when my daughter came to visit me from Sheffield, I made a point of taking her to Castle Drogo and we thoroughly enjoyed the morning.

I love the drive up from Bovey Tracey to Moretonhampstead and then on towards Drewsteignton. It was a Tuesday so there were familiar faces of volunteers to see as soon as we arrived at the Visitor Centre and chat with as we scanned our National Trust cards.

I always like meeting family members of friends and on this occasion, they got to meet one of mine, my daughter.

It felt good to be 'off duty' from volunteering, not that I minded being a volunteer at all. What I liked was chatting with the visitors and asking where they had travelled from.

 Some liked to ask questions, and some didn't. Some had visited the castle many times before. All the information was in booklets anyway, and now in colourful online guides for both the castle and gardens.

What I liked to say about the castle owner, Julius Drew, was how much he seemed to love his family. They lived in the castle, making it their home after the completion of the building work in 1926. The castle took 25 years to build with the expert help and guidance of architect Edwin Lutyens.

For the past 10 years, the castle has been refurbished and repaired to prevent leakage caused mainly by its flat roof. I enjoyed finally seeing the building with all the scaffolding and sheeting removed.

I also enjoyed sharing my experience of volunteering with my daughter and introducing her to my Tuesday group. That morning I got to see I still have fond memories of Castle Drogo and that it is one of my favourite places in Devon to visit.

Castle Drogo

Discovering a Quintessential English Village

byAudrey Cobbold

In the spring of 1996, my husband John and I decided to holiday near Dartmoor not knowing it would change our lives. We fell in love with the area and returned to Essex with an offer accepted on our new home. That quickly made decision is a story for another time.

For various reasons we couldn't move for another year; but before committing ourselves completely, we journeyed to Devon to show our fifteen-year-old son, Jonathan our new Bovey Tracey home. John's elderly mum accompanied us.

On a sunny morning, we drove out to introduce Jonathan and Mum to the wonders of Dartmoor. On the road to Becky Falls, Jonathan and I decided to leave the car to explore. We didn't intend to meet with John as we intended to return shortly.

We climbed slopes, and made our way through heathland and prickly gorse, always wanting to know what was just ahead. That was me, but I'm not so sure about Jonathan.

Eventually, we arrived upon a quiet country road which, we decided might lead somewhere interesting.

On that mid-spring afternoon, in our bid to get to that 'somewhere', it is doubtful we appreciated the scenery.

However, it was probably much as it is today. An enchantment of birdsong and primroses, with sheep grazing sleepily in the meadows with their little lambs, and what was to become my favourite spring landscape. Mauve hued trees in groups leading down the hill to a tranquil lake, and in the foreground grassy paddocks occupied by a couple of much-admired Shetland ponies, with a fluffy blue sky spread over the scene.

On that spring day, twenty-three years ago, we eventually arrived at a signpost pointing to Lustleigh. We made our way down a narrow lane, past delightful cottages; some thatched, some with flower-filled gardens and one with a small stream running through its garden.

That was how we discovered Lustleigh, a quintessential Devon village complete with a medieval church, a country pub, a village shop and thatched tearooms. While sitting in the sun, in my mind's eye I could see Miss Marple walking through the tearoom door, having enjoyed a Devon cream tea.

I was yet to discover how a walk down that road overlooking Lustleigh has the power to still my often-racing thoughts until, gazing upon a favourite landscape, my very being becomes one with that tranquil scene.

N.B. On investigating further we probably arrived at Lustleigh by the top road but the above is how I remember it.

Lustleigh

My Favourite Place in Devon –
Babbacombe
by Helen Cowell

I grew up in the lovely seaside town of Babbacombe where my parents had a guest house for many years.

One of my favourite places to visit was the beaches and the surrounding area where I spent many happy hours with my friends and Pluto, my little terrier.

We walked across Walls Hill, which is a very large green area, to reach the beautiful coastline where you can see for miles with Anstey Cove and Redgate beach on your right and Babbacombe Bay on your left.

From there, we would walk down to Babbacombe Beach. On the way, we would pass a very large house which was empty and very creepy. It was said to be haunted. As small children, we wanted to investigate, so we went up to the large heavy door. We were able to open it. It creaked very loudly with every movement as did the floor inside.

We ventured in further, but I remember being very scared in case we were locked in, so we left.

I found out later that this was where John Lee lived – the man they couldn't hang. He was thought to have murdered Emma Keyse who he worked for. He then set fire to the house. He was tried at the courts, found guilty and was sentenced to be hanged.

When he went to the gallows, he was prepared for his fate and put on the trap door. On the first attempt, the trap door did not open. They tried a second and a third time, but the door did not open, so he was sentenced to twenty-six years in prison.

He was born in Abbotskerwell. When he left school, he went to work at The Glen in Babbacombe, then he served in the Royal Navy and was known as a thief. He was invalided out, then returned to The Glen to work. The murder and failed hanging occurred after this time.

He died on March the 19th 1945 aged 80 years old, in the USA.

My favourite place in Devon
by Leighton King

You might ask what a sailboat has to do with writing about "my favourite place in Devon".

Before we were married, unknowingly, my wife and I both harboured a secret desire to sail around the world.

Our journey would begin in Devon and the River Dart.

Together, we saved enough to buy a 25-year-old ocean-going, 40-foot sailboat named Makarma ['My Karma']. It was love at first sight.

We bought Makarma in Southampton, sailed her around to Dartmouth, moored up and waited for a high spring tide so we could motor up the Dart river to Totnes for winter, haul out and complete the hundred-and-one items on the to-do list.

We spent many happy days moored in Dartmouth preparing for a voyage beyond the UK shores. Test sails to Brittany and back, sometimes involving offshore navigation in the dark. We were getting used to trusting ourselves and Makarma.

Finally, we thought it would be good to give ourselves a taste of the Atlantic and offshore ocean sailing. Before making a final decision on our direction of travel, we devised a simple plan. We would sail south 'until the butter melted' then turn **right** [to go around the world], or **left** [into the Mediterranean].

After crossing the Bay of Biscay, and experiencing 30-foot Atlantic waves(!), we abandoned the "butter test" and 'turned left' past Gibraltar and into the Med.

We would spend the next four and a half years living and exploring the Mediterranean islands and countries.

After several thousand miles we fetched up in Turkey.

Of all the amazing and beautiful places we have had the opportunity to visit, Dartmouth in Devon is still the most magical of places.

To quote Dorothy in the Wizard of OZ, "There is no place like home…"

We always thought of Dartmouth as our home, full of happy memories and certainly our most favourite place in Devon.

On Writing
by Maria Kinnersley

Words don't easily come to my lips, try as I might.

My heart bleeds for understanding, words thought
hours after.

And so I pick up my pen and write.

How I envy those whose eloquence is easy,

Who can stand and talk without pause or stammer,
while

Words don't easily come to my lips, try as I might.

My remedy is to seek the calm of my study

Gather paper, ink, and sit at my desk routinely.

And so I pick up my pen and write.

But still, I struggle, using hands in gestures

Pen abandoned as I act out those missing spaces, when

Words don't easily come to my lips, try as I might.

Even to utter those words of complaint generally

Over a product that's damaged or deadly.

And so I pick up my pen and write.

Now I have found the answer to my plight.

A salve to soothe the soul entirely.

Words don't easily come to my lips, try as I might.

And so I pick up my pen and write.

My Favourite Place in Devon
by Maria Kinnersley

I realised belatedly that this was going to be an awkward exercise for me to complete. Having lived in Devon for six years, you would think that my husband and I would have traversed the county, but life, as they say, got in the way.

Our new home needed a fair amount of work; then the pandemic swung into action and health issues, with hubby and with our dog, meant that pleasure trips have been curtailed.

But there is a place that is a favourite to me: Bovey Tracey. In many ways, it reminds me of St Ives, where I lived during part of my childhood a few years ago now. Its size means that when I do go there from Liverton, I nearly always meet someone I know. I feel comfortable here.

The people and places (like BTAT and St John's, my place of worship), have allowed me to do things that I would have never normally considered. And joining the Community Choir when I first came here has to rate as one of the happiest experiences.

I have found friends and gained confidence.

I've also found the town itself interesting, with places to walk, either in town or in the Parke Estate, being very convenient. Jessie, our little Border Terrier, has her favourite footpath there.

Then there's nothing like pootling around the different shops. The Mare and Foal is a favourite and Bovey Larder. Whilst, during conversations with people who have lived in the area for many more years than me, I have been told that the place is very different now, I like that it is still a little quirky. There is always something to see and of interest. Go, Bovey Tracey!

Green Man Festival, Bovey Tracey

PRESENTATION
FEBRUARY 2023

Exercise - Write About Cheese or Something Cheesy

A Cheesy Bovey Honeymoon
by Audrey Cobbold

On our first day in Bovey, my true love sent to me

A Cheddar he got for free.

On our second day in Bovey, my true love sent to me
Two Devon Blues

And a Cheddar he got for free.

On our third day in Bovey, my true love sent to me
Three Stinking Bishops, Two Devon Blues

And a Cheddar he got for free.

On our fourth day in Bovey, my true love sent to me
Four mouldy Stiltons, Three Stinking Bishops, Two
Devon Blues

And a Cheddar he got for free.

On our fifth day in Bovey, my true love sent to me
Five Celtic Golds.

Four mouldy Stiltons, Three Stinking Bishops, Two
Devon Blues

And a Cheddar he got for free.

On our sixth day in Bovey, my true love sent to me Six
cows a-mooing, Five Celtic Golds. Four mouldy
Stiltons, Three Stinking Bishops, Two Devon Blues

And a Cheddar he got for free.

On our seventh day in Bovey, my true love sent to me
Seven maids a-milking, Six cows a-mooing, Five Celtic
Golds. Four mouldy Stiltons, Three Stinking Bishops,
Two Devon Blues

And a Cheddar he got for free.

On our eighth day in Bovey, my true love sent to me
Eight vats a-churning, Seven maids a-milking, Six cows
a-mooing, Five Celtic Golds. Four mouldy Stiltons,
Three Stinking Bishops, Two Devon Blues

And a Cheddar he got for free.

On our ninth day in Bovey, my true love sent to me
Nine Cheshires ageing, Eight vats a-churning, Seven
maids a-milking, Six cows a-mooing, Five Celtic Golds.
Four mouldy Stiltons, Three Stinking Bishops, Two
Devon Blues

And a Cheddar he got for free.

On our tenth day in Bovey, my true love sent to me
Ten children chewing, Nine Cheshires ageing, Eight
vats a-churning, Seven maids-a-milking, Six cows a-
mooing, Five Celtic Golds. Four mouldy Stiltons,
Three Stinking Bishops, Two Devon Blues

And a Cheddar that he got for free.

A Cheesy Story (in the style of the Mr Men books)
by Brenda Heale

Mr Gordon Zolla didn't know where to turn to. He
just couldn't think straight.

Normally he was a very well-organised young man and
planned all his meals for the day first thing in the
morning, but although today had had his usual cheese
on toast for breakfast, cheese straws for elevenses then
cheese salad with extra cheese for lunch and had
planned to have cheese soufflé for dinner with a snack
of cheese and onions crisps in between those last 2
meals, the onion in the crisps obviously counting as
one of his 5 a day, he just couldn't think what to have
for his supper.

Oh dear, it was such a perplexing problem to have. It
was starting to give him a headache. "I am in a right

pickle over this," he said. Then eureka! He jumped up and gave a big cheesy grin. Of course, that was the answer. Lots of cheese and pickle sandwiches for supper. Then off to bed for a night of sweet cheesy dreams.

The Cheddar's the Thing
by Maria Kinnersley

"Why now?" croaked the woman as she viewed the man who stood at the entrance of her room. The carer had answered the door as she had left for the day and accompanied the snazzily dressed man to the living room.

"Visitor for you, Mrs M."

And there he was, her long-absent nephew.

She surveyed him with a baleful stare. Students who had had the misfortune to be in her class knew and feared that look. It appeared to have no effect on Archie.

"Hello, Auntie," he drawled. "Pleased to see me?"

She dropped her piece of rock-hard Cheddar onto the plate.

"It's been so long," she retorted, "but again I ask, why now?"

Archie gave a cheesy smile. He stood there in his shiny green suit with a bright red tie and socks and studied the elderly woman.

"You're not too friendly to your heir," he began. "I've come to ask a favour."

"If it's money, you're out of luck. I can't even afford decent cheese nowadays. I've had to sharpen my cheese knife to cut a chunk off."

She lifted said cheese up and tapped it against the plate, where it gave a chiming sound.

"No, I need somewhere to stay."

"Hmph," was the dismissive response. "I take it from that, you want bed and board."

His broad cheesy smile turned into an ingratiating one.

Silence ruled in the room, only disturbed by the ticking of the large clock hung on the wall.

"You know," she said fixing her eyes on his, "If I had had even one birthday card from you over the past twenty years, I might have given it some thought. The answer is no."

She picked up the maligned cheese and sucked the end.

"Shut the door on your way out."

Archie's smile wavered for a moment, then returned full throttle.

"What would my mother say?"

"Your mother, Paul, can say what she likes. She's like you with your insincere ways. You have only visited because you want something. Go… on your way."

With that, she picked up the cheese knife and threw it at him. There was a thud followed by a gurgling sound.

She looked at the prone body, with the fixed smile still present on his face.

"Good riddance," she said.

A Cheesy Start
by Doug Dunn

I remember once being invited to a birthday party by a boy at my infant school. I must have been six years old. There were about 15 of us sat in a room with paper and pencils being asked to draw something. A pencil!

After several minutes we showed our drawings which to me looked like rockets of various shapes.

Then my friend's dad asked us if we would like to go on a trip to the Moon! Everyone was very excited and the next thing we knew we were walking out to their garden and into a dark shed. We heard the door close and some loud noises on the outside. Were we really going to the Moon? Then after a while the noises stopped and the door opened. We stepped out into the bright sunshine and started walking around the garden.

Could that party have been the start of my life-long love of astronomy and space travel? Possibly, but in any case I am thankful for that experience created by my friend's dad.

This year, on Thursday 22 September 2022 there will be an observational evening at TAS, the Torbay Astro Society. If it is a clear night we will be entering the Torquay Grammar School observatory to look at planets and galaxies through their telescope. But if not a clear night the society is putting on short talks and presentations. The first one is mine which I have entitled 'Observational Evening on Mars'.

Can you believe we'll be going on a trip to Mars? We will be viewing the sky from an observatory on the surface of Mars. Would the night sky look any different? How long would it stay dark? Imagine looking at the Earth and Moon through the telescope!

I'm looking forward to giving this presentation and aiming to make it more of a discussion than a show. We'll be talking about Martian weather, seasons and eclipses of the Martian moons. Oh, and I'm planning to start with a rather cheesy question: 'If the Moon is made of cheddar what is Mars made of?'

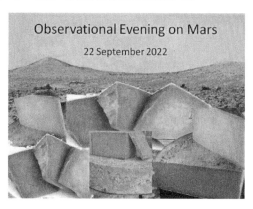

PS - I was inspired to watch another cheesy story - Wallace and Gromit in 'A Grand Day Out' written and animated by Nick Park, with the voice of Peter Sallis (Last of the Summer Wine). It was shown on Christmas Eve in 1990 and won a best Short Animation Academy Award.

Plot - very simple. They ran out of cheese, read Cheese Holiday magazine, built a spaceship to the Moon and travel there on their bank holiday. Wonderful cartoon logic!

Cheese-Cheesy-Cheesiness
by Arnold Sharpe

What a subject? What am I going to write about? I give in. I wanted to be amusing, sorry that idea failed. I looked for some kind of inspiration. Not a chance. Perspiration might bring on inspiration, no it doesn't. So, what am I left with, well, yes, cheese?

I suppose my favourite cheese is Wensleydale. A lovely crumbly hardish white cheese, a gift from the free-range well-loved cattle roaming the Yorkshire countryside. In these flat wide valleys, grass is just as green on each side of the fence. Not that I am biased in any way.

At this juncture may I give a little geography lesson. Wensleydale is the only Yorkshire dale not named after the river running through it. It is named after the village of Wensley, a small village that, if you blink your eyes, you will miss it. Not to keep those who do not know their geography in suspense, the river in Wensleydale is the Ure.

The source of the Ure is Abbotside Common, from there it travels some 74 miles before joining the Ouse. The Ouse flows through York before becoming the Humber and then on and into the North Sea. I suppose my talking about cheese ending up in a geography lesson will sound cheesy to some. I won't bore you with the many townships in the valley. Save for one, Hawes. Hawes is the home of the creamery that produces the valley's famous cheese. Visitors can gorge themselves on free nibbles.

Better still, visit on a Sunday and enjoy their Sunday Roast and their never to be beaten cauliflower cheese, to coin a phrase, to die for.

Yorkshire's broad acres can be proud of many things. Wensleydale Cheese must be high on that list.

If that last remark regarding cheese isn't cheesy enough in its cheesiness, I give up.

Cheesy
by Peter Debnam

Based on one Dictionary definition for Cheesy of 'Cheap and of low quality, unpleasant and insincere', I consider that overall our society is a reflection of this definition when compared with Britain of 50 years ago which was more like the fine wine that accompanies cheese!

Most humour today is cheesy within an ever-increasing number of comedians relying on sarcasm, nasty satire or, gyrating around the stage like Michael McIntyre, to get a laugh! Where has the hearty innocent slapstick of Ken Dodd gone?

Take the Sound of Music which I found incredibly moving and tear jerking. It was soon mocked by gangs of girls who, finding it cheesy, dressed as nuns arriving in droves at their local cinema for a sing-a-long version. In fact, the very worst example of thinking the film was cheesy was Christopher Plummer (who played Captain Von Trapp) himself, who admitted so in later years, when he called it the Sound of Mucus!

In fact, every sinew of modern day life has been infected by cheesiness. Take our politicians who regularly make insincerity their by-word with their cheesy smiles and cheap sound bites. Perhaps we could invent a new word for them 'Cheesygate' just in time for the current electoral frenzy to find our new Prime Minister. And then there's 'Political Correctness(PC)' Whilst trying to reduce mutually unacceptable behaviour, it has instead had the effect through overtly using cheesy advertising and making endless public statements of eliminating all opposition to its ideals. Much of this 'PC' has resulted in us no longer being able to say what we think without being taken to task by some Quango or other. You may think by now that I'm a miserable old sod - Victor Meldrew comes to mind - especially if you're from a younger generation. But really I'm not, it's because what is 'cheesy' to me is perfectly legitimate to them. In other words, cheesiness is really a subjective and generational issue entirely dependent upon one's perspective.

Exercise - Write About Your Favourite Object

Something I Would Hate to Lose
by Arnold Sharpe

I sit looking at the blank screen. I have a problem. I was asked to write about an object that I treasured and would hate to lose. I look around the room and see nothing. No family heirlooms, no treasured keepsakes, no nothing. I glance up at the wall facing me and suddenly realise that my most treasured possessions are the pictures looking back at me. They say nothing but speak volumes in memories. My family, my dogs, my interests and a little of my history.

One picture in particular, a black and white photograph, dated 4th December 1939, stands out and always draws my interest. Twelve faces stare stoically into the camera, not smiling, which was the fashion of the day. Standing third from the left, in the back row my mother looks down at me, my guess would be she was about 34 years old at the time of the photograph. It would be a further two years before I would appear on the scene, a war baby and not a little unexpected.Alongside my mother, both sitting and standing, her nine siblings, six sisters and three brothers. My mother was the second eldest.

In prime position and making up the numbers my Grandparents Joseph and Margaret Slater. The picture was taken in Ferryhill, County Durham. What makes it special is that it was the one and only occasion in their life that my Grandparents had their whole family together in the same place at the same time.

I occasionally look at the photograph and let my mind wander. How families separate and take different courses. Not always by choice. Being a large mining family, living in a back-to-back miner's cottage, the elder daughters had to move out to make room for the younger members coming along. With little or no work and opportunities locally for girls, the girls had to move away. The boys on the other hand were expected to go down the pit and earn money. Not all the family followed these rules but for the most part they did.

That's why I was born in Yorkshire. I have upwards of twenty-five cousins spread far and wide, some in this country, others as far away as Australia, New Zealand and the USA. I know some a little, some quite well and some not at all. In truth, I've met none of them for many years. As I finish my little piece, I look up at the photograph once again and thank my grandparents for kicking my mother out of their nest. That one act is why I am writing this exercise for you now.

My Essential Item
by Maria Kinnersley

When I look around my home at all the wonderful things I have and ponder a time in my youth when we weren't blessed with all the gadgets to help us that we have now, you'd think I'd be spoilt for choice. Yet there is a little item I would never want to be without. It is a crochet hook.

Now you may think that it's a weird item to choose but consider for a moment what makes it so useful. Yes, I can crochet items and have constructed chair backs, shawls and waistcoats for myself and my family. But there is so much more that it can be used for.

It can repair pulled stitches by threading them through to the inside of a garment, so the loose thread is no longer visible. When I sew it's invaluable for ensuring that any corners are crisp, so that shirt collars, for example, look smart.

You can also use it on paper to make a definite fold. So, it's useful for origami and card making.

It doesn't stop there. It can get into crevices and, because of the hook, I can pick up small things that have dropped into awkward places, providing they have something that can be hooked, like a loop. The list goes on. I recently found a new use for it. It's great for getting the fluffy, hard to reach, bits from a tumble dryer when cleaning that piece of equipment out.

I'm always finding new uses for it, and I'd be lost without my crochet hook. And yes, I have a set of them all in different sizes.

Something I Cannot Live Without
by Trudy Abbott

There are some things I literally cannot live without. These include oxygen in the air, food and water. I need clothing, warmth and shelter, and enough money to pay for all these things.

It would be nice to have good health, but many manage to live without it.

As the subject is personal, 'Something I cannot live without', my response might well be one of choice, rather than necessity.

It has been written that when all else passes away there will remain faith, hope and love, and that the greatest of these is love, which will go on forever. It is the theme probably of the majority of poems, and songs, many of which tell of the wretched effects of its loss, and it is what I will choose not to live without.

Love gives a deep sense of purpose in the lives of those who feed recipients of an adequate amount of it.

How can it be defined, and how can we possible ensure we will always experience enough of it in a world where the pain of rejection is all too commonplace?

Pure love has been defined as patience, gentleness, kindness, self-control, and is forgiving. It is not jealous or boastful or rude, nor is it irritable, or demanding of its own way, or selfish. It isn't haughty, and does not hold grudges, or easily take offence. It is never glad about injustice, but rejoices when truth wins its way. It cannot be bought. It is loyal, believes in us and expects the best of us. It does not depend on any acceptable level of deservedness on the part of the recipient. It can be found in chemistry, and expressed in the giving of gifts, words of affirmation, a tender touch of understanding, and in acts of service.

How can we possibly find this pure love in a constant form in any human being? I don't believe we can! Such sublime affection can only possibly be an attribute of a higher being, the earnest search for whom, I believe, will never know disappointment.

My Fuji Camera
by Doug Dunn

Dear Fuji,

I have been asked to write about my favourite object and I have decided to choose you! Sorry for not using your full name Fujifilm FinePix 5200EXR. My memory is failing, unlike yours which holds every photo I have taken with you for the last thirteen years.

I felt honoured when you were given to me by a dear friend Ed, an experienced photographer whom I regard as a kind of father figure. Well, I did until I regrettably misled his phone number and lost touch with him. I fear the worst, but yesterday I wrote Ed an email thanking him for giving me a camera. He could have sold or given you to someone else. So that makes you a special object to me.

You have been with me Fuji on several trips abroad from Romania to Malawi, France, New York, Vancouver and California. 1700 images on a single memory card so easy to view and save on my laptop and share with others, including my Writing for Pleasure group!

I enjoyed using you for my Mill Marsh Park Tree Trail presentation for BTAT last year. It was fun and might have encouraged people to use their cameras and make presentations.

While I take everyday pictures with my phone I love that you have extra features like a 14x zoom magnification which is good for bird photography. Then allowing shutter speeds of up to 30 seconds is perfect for photographing stars and planets. That's when I attach you to my tripod in places like Haytor car park. I also like that you have extra settings still to be discovered for increasing depth, sharpness and picture quality.

This morning I received a reply from Ed's daughter Pamela. She wrote that sadly her father passed away in May 2020 after an illness. I feel very sad but glad I got to know what happened through writing this letter.

Thank you, Fuji.

Best regards with many more to come, Doug

PS see the very first picture I took of Ed back in 2009.

Ed Pinto

The item I would never be without
by Peter Debnam

You would think that a titanium plate in my upper left arm would hardly be the item to be the one I choose never to be without. Let me explain: 40 years of accident-free skiing and I break my arm not on the piste but falling backwards down a restaurant's marble staircase which I was unaware was immediately behind me! Little did I realise at the time that this event was to have such a profound and sustaining effect on my life.

After the immediate shock and pain, I quickly recognised my good fortune of not having broken my right user arm, nor had my back taken the impact and head against marble would have meant my not being with you here today.

I witnessed the tremendous skill and kindness at the clinic who returned me to my Tyrolean hotel within 36 hours – plus fully mended arm! Back home I needed physiotherapy not for my arm, but for my left shoulder which had been badly compressed when I hit the marble. I was unable to elevate my arm above waist level but my Physiotherapist injected in me not with medication but an absolute certainty that my shoulder would heal. And so it happened after an hour a day exercise every day for five months, I could finally lift a cup off the top shelf of the kitchen cabinet! Yes this lesson clearly taught me greater spatial awareness, but far greater was my emerging understanding that negativity merely reflects your mind's historical perspective of life situations: an erroneous absolute position simply requiring an adjustment of one's perspective.

The even broader question posed is whether events such as I have described are allowed or even meant to occur by spiritual forces beyond our understanding which enable us to move to a higher human state. But that weighty question I will leave the reader to ponder for another day.

Decision: Enrico Caruso or a Tea Set by Audrey Cobbold

My mum met my dad while waiting for a bus on a rainy day in Dublin. He asked her if she would like to shelter under his umbrella. They married secretly seven months later – not as romantic as it sounds. They had a private wedding, in a Methodist church, with only my dad's sister and brother-in-law as witnesses. My mum was marrying out of her Jewish religion.

My dad was the youngest of a large family and had become their housekeeper as his father had died before he was born and his mother had died when he was about fourteen. So, while the rest of the family made their way in the world, he did the cooking and cleaning. When my mum told her parents she had secretly married a non-Jew, they disowned her.

My dad set about looking for his first job and they found a small flat. I was the youngest, and by the time I was born, we were living in a corporation house on the outskirts of Dublin; my dad had a job working in the showrooms of a house decorators in town. It was poorly paid, and money was scarce.

Dad loved classical music and I grew up to the sound of Enrico Caruso and Kathleen Ferrier. When I was nine or ten they were about to celebrate their 25th wedding anniversary. My dad had a dilemma; how could he afford the beautiful Royal Grafton bone china tea set he had seen in a Dublin department store.

Dad had a much-treasured collection of Caruso records. It was the only thing of any value he had to sell; so he sold them to pay for the tea set. Was there ever a gift given with more love? My mum treasured this wonderful tea set for the rest of her life, but was cross at the time because she knew the sacrifice dad had made to buy it.

Dad died when I was fourteen; my mum when our children were in their teens. Now looking at this amazing tea set as I type, I remember well days gone by and the love my parents shared.

Exercise - Write About Packing a Suitcase

Happenings in the Suitcase
by Michael Dudley

No matter if I'm packing my suitcase for a weekend away, or for a fortnight's holiday, I always have to leave space inside for a certain traveller who won't let me close up without packing him in.

Yes, my Teddy Bear insists on travelling everywhere with me, and has to be last in and first out. Yemmy loves to travel by suitcase. He loves the helter-skelter of the suitcase transportation system, and he likes the chatter of all the other Teddies and other stuffed toys packed in the other luggage travelling on the conveyors. Newer travellers get sick sometimes, which causes the 'old paws' some amusement.

None of them like it when everything comes to a halt for they all have to wait, sometimes for long periods, and then they often wish that the suitcase had been packed with more **care.**

But Yemmy takes it all in his stride. After all, he's been travelling for more than 30 years!!

We Are Suitcases!
by Peter Debnam

'Well, what a place to meet! I find these airport customs halls so joyless and uninviting.'

'Exactly, and yet we've been left here by both our owners after such humiliating searches. I must have been rifled through for at least half an hour and what did they find – absolutely nothing! I'm Sam, by the way, and we're headed for Malaga, what about you?'

'Oh, I'm Susan and we're off to St Moritz but I have to say that I was only rummaged through for about 2 minutes so I can't really complain. I'm not really sure why I was opened in the first place after the amount of care my folks took to pack me?'

'Ah, maybe that had something to do with it as I can assure you my folks took hours and could never agree what was to go and what wasn't and how it should be packed – a nightmare!'

'Poor Sam, do you mean whether it should be folded or rolled?'

'Folded or rolled, that's hilarious! They just chucked it in and boy did it smell. They hadn't washed much of it! Also, clothing items were added and then removed numerous times as they battled over individual supremacy of what was going!'

'Oh, didn't they write a list of what to take and agree on beforehand? My folks always sit down at the kitchen table and talk things through, often adding or deleting items to achieve a mutual agreement. Mother insists on washing all clothing to be packed and then deciding whether to fold it or roll it. The heavier items, like hand towels, are best rolled and the rest folded. You can get much more in me that way, Sam.'

'Maybe Susan, but they always put too much in, then close me up and weigh me. They soon realise that they're overweight – pardon the pun! - and I hear the muffled sounds of shouting and screaming as I am frogmarched into the bedroom where I am literally thrown onto the bed, re-opened and the endless cycle of packing continued!'

'Poor Sam, how simply ghastly! Well, at least you'll enjoy sunny Spain, unlike me freezing in Switzerland!'

Packing a Suitcase
by Brenda Heale

It's quite a big suitcase so I'll be able to get a fair bit inside. It's just deciding what are the best pieces to take with me as I've only a limited time to pack. Let's have a look around.

Those expensive new trainers of course, still unpacked from their box, and the Channel suit that hangs in the wardrobe and the Armani one. Yes, I know neither looks good with the trainers, but they are classic styles that never go out of fashion.

The designer handbags of course. Gucci and Prada. I love those, and there are a few others. Why choose? Take them all if they will fit in. I can always sit on top of the case at the end to press things down and help get it shut.

Jewellery – now that must be here somewhere. Where has the jewellery box gone? Ah, here it is. Lovely great rings with diamonds amethyst and rubies. What about the tiara? An occasion for someone to wear that might arise and it is so pretty and sparkly. Earrings, bracelets. They will fit easily in between, and the gold Rolex watch of course. That looks good with anything.

How's the time going? Nearly time to go on my journey I think. Better pop in a few bits of the family silver. That's traditional for a burglary, isn't it? And I like to do things proper, and off I go through the window that was conveniently left open. Wish me luck!!

Packing is so Final
by Maria Kinnersley

Penny gazed down at her case, gaping like an open mouth waiting to be filled. She shivered. Why did I think a pink lining would be attractive she thought?

There was so little time to pack. Andrew would be back in less than an hour.

She shook herself. Time to get on with it. But what to take?

At a run, she moved to the bathroom and grabbed her wash bag, toothbrush and paste. He'd have to get his own. He was always telling her he didn't like Colgate. Now's the time to choose your own, she thought grimly.

That was the easy part. She considered the next stage as she rolled the bathroom items in a clean towel.

Seizing the top drawer in the dressing table, she tipped the contents into the case next to the towel package. Then she opened the wardrobe and stared at its contents. With a glance at what she was currently wearing, she slipped a couple of blouses from their hangers, snatched a pair of jeans and rifled through the shelves for T-shirts and fleece.

Bending forward, Penny picked up her trainers and a pair of low-heeled shoes. Turning to the case she added the clothes without ceremony. She paused her eyelids flickered as she listened. No, that wasn't his car.

The lid fastened, she gripped the handle, shouldered her handbag, ran down the stairs and out the door. She didn't want to be there when he returned. It was one affair too many.

Packing My Suitcase Without Regrets
by Doug Dunn

While driving up the motorway on route for a family walking weekend in the Yorkshire Dales, I started doing my usual thing; thinking what have I forgotten to pack in my suitcase?

On one trip abroad I had forgotten my passport and quickly did a U-turn. So, on that occasion it was good to do a mental checklist.

But on this trip there was nothing urgent missing and no time for turning back anyway. So I stopped thinking about that and any regrets about what I'd forgotten to pack.

Then, I wondered if this might be a pattern I had developed. Where else did I have regrets? A common one is what I wish I had said. 'Why didn't I say that?' What I 'can' say is how proud I am of my son being a music composer and my daughter for buying her first house. I can say how wonderful they have both grown up to be.

I'm back home now and we are having fun sending each other photos of the places we visited. We saw waterfalls at Aysgarth, bought Wensleydale cheese and ginger parkin at Hawes, visited Richmond castle and walked in a nature reserve near Grassington. These were all suggested by a fellow Writing for Pleasure member (Arnold) and I am pleased to have packed so much into one weekend. We had a lovely time with some good conversations, and I definitely have no regrets!

Bolton Castle, Wensleydale

Packing a Suitcase
by Arnold Sharpe

Packing a suitcase is not a gift. Packing a suitcase is not an art. Packing a suitcase is not a science. Packing can be a solo or team sport.

Why? I ask, pack a suitcase at all. Why anyone wishes to travel abroad in times like these is quite puzzling. The airports are a nightmare, even William Hill will not give you odds against your flight taking off. To add insult to injury the airport authorities and airlines herd their customers like cattle and treat them with total disdain. They feel that explaining the delays and cancellations and why they have occurred, is not necessary.

It used to be sea sickness that was a main drawback to ferry travel, now it is the interminable waits to board the ferry, followed by the ridiculous delays at passport control.

Add to this the threat of industrial action and the continual shaming by the carbon footprint brigade on to what we are inflicting on the world.

We should walk everywhere! Electricity comes from the sun and grows on trees! I repeat, why travel abroad?

Staycations fare no better. Traffic jams on the roads, cancelations and delays on the railways. This is after taking into consideration the price of fuel and the exorbitant price of rail fares.

Sorry, I digress. I started writing about packing a suitcase and seem to have drifted out on a tangent. As usual.

Back to packing a suitcase.

First, pick the size of suitcase needed.

Second, place the case at a height that will not cause back injuries.

Third, it helps if the packer has a rough idea as to what will be required when reaching their destination. As a norm, far more clothing is packed than is required. This should be a major consideration and accordingly, action should be taken.

Fourth, the packer usually ignores the third piece of advice. This can lead to excess weight allowance and the extra cost involved and back injuries to whoever is carrying the suitcase.

Fifth, when closing the packed suitcase help may be needed to secure the fastenings. If care is taken this can be done without injury.

If there have been no falling outs, this augurs well for the forthcoming journey.

Caution, packing can stretch relationships.

Beware, pulled muscles can spoil a holiday.

As previously stated, packing is not a gift, not an art, not a science. But packing can be a pain in the backside.

Story Prompt

Your main character is a bus driver. The bus driver has finished a long shift and driven their bus back to the depot. Before leaving to go home, they are required to clean their bus so it will be ready for them when they return to work in the morning. In doing so, they find something unexpected.

The Bus Driver (The Orb)
by Peter Denham

What he saw surprised even Dave who was used to seeing most detritus of humanity at the end of a day on the buses. But this glowing orb he knew was something very special. His first thoughts were how did it get there in the first place and to whom did it belong and of course, what did it do and why was he chosen to find it, if indeed he was?

His first thoughts were to hand it in as lost property, but that little voice within him told him to keep it, at least for a short while. He was an honest and simple fellow and quite poor, relatively speaking as he had never acquired any real wealth to speak of, not like you saw constantly displayed on our TV screens anyway.

He trotted off home to his wife who gave the orb a quick polish before they sat down for tea. They engaged on a lengthy discussion about the orb before a very tired Dave fell asleep on the sofa.

The next morning, his wife found Dave already up and busy weeding the garden. It was only 7 am! What was going on? He explained to his wife that he couldn't ever recall having felt such a passion to beautify the garden.

As the day went on, Dave experienced a joy in everything he did, including all those little tasks that he had previously found a chore or paid someone else to do.

His previous feelings of resentment and jealousy of those who had much more material wealth simply dissipated as he began to understand that he had this overwhelming feeling of inner contentment; that his lot in life was where he was now and it was a truly wonderful feeling.

By the end of the day, his wife was also following the same path of inner joy and they both realised it had to be connected to the orb, but how? They both approached the orb which was sitting on the kitchen table. They felt it but nothing appeared to happen, it simply continued to emit a soft amber glow.

Dave's wife decided to check the definition of orb in the family dictionary and read that it was 'a symbol of the cosmos, or of the universe as a harmonious whole.'

They agreed that they both now felt such harmony, but why them?

To be continued!

Found on the Bus
by Brenda Heale

"Boring Brian" or "Book face Brian" - they were two of the more bearable nicknames he had acquired at school.

Brian's mother had not given birth to him until she was halfway through her 40s and had given up on the idea of ever being able to reproduce.

Brian's father was strict but distant. Distant both in manner when he was at home and by the fact he seldom was there anyway.

Brian spent his childhood with his nose in a book. He made few friends and went on to get a sensible job as a bus driver. The country buses he usually drove were mainly used by pensioners with their free bus passes. So, he was quite happy with that.

There was one horrific fortnight when he was put driving the school bus as the usual driver was off sick. Those were the worst two weeks of his life with all those noisy, boisterous, free-range kids; but thankfully he was back on his normal routes now.

One of the things he liked best about these runs was, with many of the people who used the bus being of a more mature age range, there was not so much cleaning up to do at the end of his shift as their generation didn't seem to leave behind the trail of rubbish that the younger ones did.

On this day, there was an abandoned newspaper. Not today's and only a tabloid, so he wouldn't take that home to read later, and a few other pieces of paper together with some wrappers from Werther's Originals.

Scooping the bits and pieces into his bin Brian spotted a lottery ticket.

"What a waste of money," he said as he examined it briefly.

He realised it was for that evening's lottery. He'd refused to join the other bus drivers in their syndicate of lottery tickets. The odds were too much against winning for Brian to partake in such nonsense, though the other drivers had scoffed when he told them this and called him an old skinflint.

He put the ticket into his pocket anyway and decided to watch the results later to check it out.

His wife Shirley was surprised to find him watching for the lottery results that evening.

"What's it to us Brian?" she said. "You never buy a ticket. You're too much of a mean boring old sod to do that."

He wasn't sure why, but he didn't tell her about finding the ticket in the rubbish. The numbers came up. 3, 26. He saw he had both of those, then 46. Three numbers... that was a small win wasn't it? He wasn't sure. Then his other numbers were read out and then the bonus number. Brian was dumbstruck. Could that have really happened?

"Shirley," he shouted, "I've won."

But she didn't reply. She was too busy watching last night's 'Strictly Come Dancing' again on catch-up in the other room.

An unusual idea started to form in Brian's mind. He checked how much he was likely to win. Well over two million pounds.

"I'll claim no publicity," he thought, "and Shirley and my work colleagues can hear about my windfall when I phone them from the holiday home I'll buy in the Bahamas. Not so much boring Brian now, is it?" he grinned as he looked on line at a selection of expensive suitcases.

The Legend of "Bus Puss"
By Leighton King

A children's story (with participation) for Allegra, age 3-3/4

At the end of each shift, it was the responsibility of the driver to tidy up the bus before handing it over to the next driver.

As my sweeping reached the back of the bus, I looked under the last seat and to my surprise, there was something under the seat looking back at me.

It was a surprise to both of us. There was a rather large cat gazing back at me.

"Hello," I said, "what are you doing under the seat on my bus?"

The cat shrunk back further into the corner.

"It's okay, I'm not going to hurt you."

I thought maybe it would come out from underneath the seat if I tempted it with something to eat or drink.

In the depot, there was a room for the drivers to have coffee and prepare for the next shift. I went in and found a small container, filled it with milk and a crushed up digestive biscuit. When I returned to the bus, I found that the cat had not budged an inch. I placed the milk and biscuit just out of the cat's reach and backed away to watch.

The cat must have been really thirsty because it went straight for the milk and lapped it up in seconds!!

Then the cat spoke. "Gosh, that was good. Thank you."

WHAT! A talking cat! Stunned, I asked, "What are you doing on my bus?"

The cat reached behind and produced a baton which he raised above his head, and suddenly everyone in the bus depot felt the urge to sing… (Everyone participates)

"The wheels on the bus go round and round, round and round, round and round. The wheels on the bus go round and round… all day long."

The cat made a decisive snap of the baton and the singing stopped.

The cat spoke, "Thanks for the milk and biscuit mate. This is my stop."

The cat walked to the door of the bus and hopped down onto the pavement. Before he disappeared into the crowd, I shouted, "Who are you?"

The cat looked back. "That's easy. I'm Bus Puss, one of the last of the great bus conductors."

Message Misunderstood
by Maria Kinnersley

"Now what's this?" Vera murmured as she spied a white square caught on the trim of one of the seats.

She struggled with her conscience. Should she investigate or just finish and go home? Only the fact that she'd been given an official warning for 'poor cleaning practices' this week forced her to bend forward and examine the mysterious object further.

She reached down and tugged. The slip of paper came away and she gazed at the words.

I KNOW WHERE YOU WERE LAST SUMMER

Vera's casual glance became fixed. Her other hand went to her mouth.

"No," she whispered. "He can't have. How did it get here?"

There was a pause as she frowned, deep in thought.

"Who's told him?"

Only this week he'd proposed to her. She'd joyfully accepted. If he knows, she thought, then it's off.

He knew she had gone on a singles holiday, but Vera kept to herself what happened. She'd suspected he might be ready to ask for her hand in marriage, so took the opportunity to make the most of those good-looking, pleasure-loving males that were there. Women can sow wild oats too she thought.

Now her face felt frozen into the despair she felt as she stood with the damning note.

A movement on the steps made her jump. A head peeped around the screen. He was panting.

"Oh, I'm so glad I've caught you."

She stared at him, dumbstruck.

"Have you come across a slip of paper?"

She raised it.

"That's the one!"

He came forward and held out his hand. It dropped from her nerveless fingers onto his palm.

"Thank you for finding it. It's the name of a film my girlfriend wants to see. Apparently, it's highly recommended."

With a nod, he left the bus as she gawped after him.

The Bus That Wasn't a Home
by Audrey Cobbold

Mike was at the end of his shift driving a double-decker bus from Newquay to Truro. The cleaners were on strike so he would have to clean it before he went home, but first he was desperate to use the loo.

It was pouring down with rain, and he was in such a hurry that he had left the bus without locking up. When he got on board to clean up he found he was not alone. There were two very wet children inside the bus and an equally wet man in the driving seat. To his surprise he recognised the man. He was Martin Brown who used to work as a bus driver for the bus company, until his wife sadly died, and he had to look after his children. Mike judged them to be about five and seven.

It looked very much like Martin was about to drive the bus off.

"What's going on," shouted Mike.

"Hello Mike," exclaimed Martin blushing bright crimson. "I'm afraid I'm very much down on my luck. I was thrown out of our home because I was badly in arrears with the mortgage what with interest rates going up not to mention everything else, we didn't stand a chance, especially as I couldn't even get a job that fitted in with school hours. We were given a room in a dingy hotel miles away from the children's school but it didn't work out."

"I'm sorry to hear that, but what are you doing in the bus at this late hour," questioned Mike.

"I was going to drive it into the woods behind the children's school. I helped a friend convert an old bus into a holiday home a couple of years ago. I thought I could repaint the outside so no one would be any the wiser. Mike, you could say it was stolen. I have the knowhow to convert it into a temporary home. I could buy what I need from charity shops."

"Martin, that's a mad plan. I could lose my job and you might end up in prison."

Martin got up. "Come on kids lets go." The desperation was in his voice.

Mike was suddenly reminded of something he had pushed to the back of his mind; he had got into trouble when he was a lad. He was drinking heavily and getting off his face on drugs. His dad had chucked him out and he could have ended up dead in a doorway if someone hadn't decided he was worth helping.

By this time Martin and his kids had left the bus.

"Wait," he shouted running after them."You can stay with me until you sort something more permanent out. I have the room, Maggie and I are divorced, and she has moved to Scotland with her new bloke, so I don't have the kids to stay very often. My nephew works in Tesco. He was telling me they were looking for people to stack shelves in the early hours. You might be in with a chance, people don't like unsocial hours. I don't start work until eleven in the morning so I could look after the kids. Come on Martin. I'll lock the bus and we will be on our way."

The Number 88 From Middleham
by Arnold Sharpe

(The new Detective Inspector Fynn Mystery)

Prologue

Wearily Joe pulled the wheel over and steered the bus over the forecourt and into the depot. The end of a seven- hour shift. No, he thought not quite the end. His contract stated that he must leave the bus in a clean and presentable condition ready for the next day's first journey. This shouldn't take much time and, looking at his watch there should be time for a quick pint or two at The Goats Head before last orders were called.

He heaved his overweight body out of the driver's seat; he stretched his arms and legs and patted his stomach. His smile broadened as he thought of Elizabeth, at home, preparing his late supper. The diet he kept promising himself would have to wait another week.

He smiled again, after this evening's shift ended, he would not be back on duty for five days. A day's fishing was high on his to do list, the pike that had slipped off his hook last week was still waiting for him. First, he would have to earn some brownie points. Finishing that decorating job in the back bedroom would be a good start.

Joe collected his brush and cleaning gear and as usual would commence the cleaning on the upper deck. The on-bus security cameras had shown nothing of note over the ten return trips he had driven to and from Middleham. He had not had any drunks or other disturbances on board; in fact, the majority of his passengers had been pensioners taking advantage of their bus passes. Without these old fogies, he thought, he would be driving around in an empty bus with the possibility of the bus company going out of business.

He was not completely alone in the garage; he waved at two of his colleagues finishing their shifts. He climbed the stairs to the upper deck and began tidying up. He heard a sound from behind him, swinging round he could see nothing.

Shrugging his shoulders, he continued with his task. Another sound. This time when he turned around a shadow had materialised out of seemingly nowhere.

"What the hell," he said and stopped.

A knife appeared in the shadow's hand and with surprising speed plunged into his stomach. His last thoughts as the darkening mists descended, were bugger, there goes my fishing, my pint and

Elizabeth's supper…………..

Poetry (the first time attempted in this group)

The End of the Day
by Michael Dudley

The sky seems to hold its breath
at dusk when the sun is setting
it's as though it's afraid
that the sun may crash
instead of sinking into the west
signalling the end of the day.

The clouds, which half an hour ago
were rushing across the sky
as though they had to get somewhere
are now stationary
in silent salute
to the signal for the end of the day.

Mrs Armstrong's Class
by John Beech

We pulled faces,
Behind her back.
"Beech!" – Maria said,
"I Love You!"
It took me (aback)

No one said, "I Love You!" (before)
I'll always wonder,
What it meant,
Why me adore?

Innocent Love
Girls were taboo.
The memory lingers,
Does yours too?

Now I'm married,
Settled at last,

I still wonder
About the past.

T'was a blur,
What happened then,
A girl's voice-,
"I love you!"
Breaks through again!

What really happened?
I'll never know,
Over the years,
Across the miles,
The secrets buried,
Under time's snow!

Poems
by Leighton King

Mirror:
Silver shadow on the wall
Sees nothing
Reflects all

The Oracle:
Religion became the last centre of repose
Without which, man was but a shadow
And his very existence
As meaningless as the leaves
the Sybil scattered in the wind

Mitch Miller's sign off:
Be kind to your web-footed friends
For a duck maybe somebody's mother
Be kind to your friends in the swamp
Where the weather is very, very damp
Well you may think this is the end

Well it is.

Write a Poem She Said
by Arnold Sharpe

'Write a poem' she said. It may help in developing your writing. After three weeks the only thing I've developed is a headache.

'Write a poem' she said. Look out at what you see around you, take note and compose. After running out of pencils and paper, I am not composed, agitated perhaps, frustrated for sure.

'Write a poem' she said. Listen, she said, to the sounds that surround you. Birdsong, the rustle of autumn leaves beneath your feet. So far, this autumn, the rain has taken all the rustle out of a woodland walk and the birds seem more intent on taking shelter and my deaf aid needs new batteries.

'Write a poem' she said. Maybe a sonnet or a limerick or if you wish a haiku. To the uninitiated like myself, a haiku is a Japanese form of poetry. Those who are versed, yes, I mean versed, in creativity, seem to think there is a potential William Wordsworth lurking behind every daffodil. I am still seeking that daffodil to lurk behind.

'Write a poem' she said. So far, I have come to the conclusion that to write a poem one needs flair, a commodity I seem to have a great shortage of.

'Write a poem' she said. She asked for it. So, after hours of navel gazing here goes. With my apologies to all poets both the living and the dead.

This month's task, is to write a rhyme,

Your subject shall be Devon,

Breathe in breathe out and take your time,

Just imagine you're in Heaven.

From Devon's shores to moorland Tors,

People in their thousands flock.

They suffer holdups and delays,

To wonder at our granite rock.

From Yorkshire, a 'blow in' I am called,

Me, a grockle? no longer can they claim.

My goods and chattel I have hauled,

To live my life in Devon is now my only aim.

Exercise - Pick a cliché. Write for it or against it, or even both.

Confused.com
by Arnold Sharpe

Pick a cliché. Write for it or against it, or even both. That was September's topic. I was chomping at the bit but unfortunately, I got distracted and went off at a tangent.

What is a cliché? Trying not to be a bull in a china shop, my research led to idioms. 'Under the weather' I am told, is an idiom meaning feeling unwell. Yet, 'Fresh as a daisy' meaning feeling well is a cliché, not an idiom.

Am I splitting hairs here, let's get this clear. A cliché is a phrase or opinion that is over used and betrays a lack of original thought. Surly idioms should be tarred with the same brush.

In the beginning all clichés must have been original, as is the case for idioms. Therefore, when idioms are overused, why do they not morph into clichés?

I find myself between a rock and a hard place here, and it goes beyond the pale that nothing is done to rectify this anomaly. At this moment in time, I can see no immediate answer and I seem to be banging my head against a brick wall which makes my blood boil.

By the same token, by hook and by crook, come hell or high water, this anomaly must be clarified. Why, I ask should a cliché play second fiddle to an idiom.

Am I out on a limb here? Have I opened a can of worms? I may even have bitten off more than I can chew but I refuse to sit on the fence.

To add insult to injury, clichés remain the poor relation of idioms. Not to beat around the bush, at the end of the day we have to weather the storm and take the bull by the horns. It will not be as easy as pie to see this through to a conclusion.

Bringing my tirade to an end, I do not wish to be a pain in the neck and go off like a loose cannon. By the same token some of my readers may think that I am barking up the wrong tree. They may think that I am flogging a dead horse and that my arguments fall as flat as a pancake.

Going forward, I hope to weather the storm and have everyone singing from the same hymn sheet.

Last but not least. Both idioms and clichés remain forces to be reckoned with and without them our prose would be as clear as mud.

At this moment in time a cliché remains a cliché, an idiom remains an idiom. Possibly ne'er the twain shall meet. For all intents and purposes, the devil is in the detail.

At the end of the day, should I get off my high horse and let sleeping dogs lie?

A Stitch in Time Saves Nine
by Sheila Winckles

This saying takes me back to my childhood. My mother was always keen that my sister and I should never sit idle during the evening when we were listening to the radio, so she taught us how to knit jumpers and cardigans for ourselves. This was never a chore to us because it meant we finished with a garment in the colour we liked, and we hadn't had to spend our precious clothing coupons.

My mother also had an old Singer sewing machine which I liked to use to make clothes for my dolls. As I grew older sewing became the activity I really enjoyed. I used to make most of my dresses and when I got married made my bride's dress and my bridesmaids' dresses as well as curtains and cushions etc for my new home.

One of my daughters became a keen seamstress from a young age and always enjoyed sewing on my machine. Sometimes it was a case of who set it up first! But now I am so proud of her because she runs her own design business. They have contracts with such companies as Disney to copy their fashions as shown in films for children to wear. So whenever one of us says we are sewing at home, I hear my mother saying to either my sister or myself when we complained that there was a hole in our clothes or socks that needed darning:

"A stitch in time saves nine."

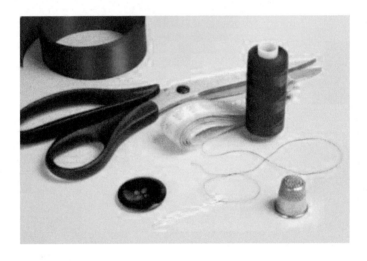

Nothing Ventured Nothing Gained
by Doug Dunn

What is the point of clichés? Should writers avoid them like the plague? Sorry, there's another one. Or could they ever be useful to the reader?

I think an inspiring cliché is 'Nothing ventured, nothing gained'. I have found it useful recently when trying to make up my mind about making a decision. This one involved attending an online course which possibly will include travel to a new country. But the cliché could equally apply to learning a new language, starting a new relationship or playing a musical instrument. Not too sure about the last one, though music has taken my composer son to visit many places around the world. At a recent family wedding I attended, he entertained a room full of people by playing familiar songs and even getting us to sing along.

Through this cliché I have decided to join a small group of people and connect with them for five weekends over a period of half a year starting this October. Wow! I feel happy with my decision. We will be 'zooming' online, supporting each other in what we are up to and hopefully having some fun. Similar to our writing for pleasure group! I would love my online group to meet up at the end to celebrate what we have achieved: what we have gained through venturing out together.

After writing this I did meet up with my group on the first weekend back in October. One of the questions we looked into was 'Who are we when we walk into a room?' It was an interesting question which I answered with including everyone and listening fully to them.

At the end of that day, I was invited to a birthday party by my group facilitator. Though at first, I was reluctant to go out after a long day, I remembered 'nothing ventured, nothing gained' and that I could put into practice walking into a new room! The party was a lot of fun and what I gained was meeting some very lovely people.

Cliché – Raining Cats and Dogs
by Maria Kinnersley

I think that until I brought up the subject of clichés at the last meeting, I hadn't fully appreciated how much our speech is governed by them. When I mentioned to my husband that we had talked about clichés he spent the next few hours with a cliché coming up every few minutes. It was exhausting. (He's still doing it!)

And I spent a lot of time reading through the different lists found on the Internet. I finally concluded that while some appear to make sense there is a corresponding number which had me scratching my head. And raining cats and dogs is one of them.

The visual image of dogs and cats falling from the sky doesn't immediately bring to mind a heavy downpour, and yet, that is what it is associated with. Its origins are dim and distant. They don't really know who first coined the phrase. Two quotes have been mentioned coming from Jonathan Swift.

Sweeping from Butchers Stalls, Dung, Guts, and Blood, Drown'd Puppies, stinking Sprats, all drench'd in Mud, Dead Cats and Turnip-Tops come tumbling down the Flood. (Tatler Magazine 1710)

"I know Sir John will go, though he was sure it would rain cats and dogs" (A Complete Collection of Polite and Ingenious Conversation 1738).

It is not clear whether he was alluding to streets flowing with dead cats and dogs swept into the River Fleet during heavy rain bearing in mind the conditions of the roads and the lack of drainage or that he was the one who coined the phrase.

Then we have a quote from Richard Brome: -

"It shall raine... Dogs and Polecats" (The City Wit or The Woman wears the Breeches 1653) which specifically refers to stormy weather.

Other suggestions go back to Norse mythology where dogs attended Odin, the god of storms. Witches had cats as familiars and are supposed to have ridden the wind, but there is no firm evidence that the cliché dates back that far.

There are some who say that it comes from a version of the French word catadupe meaning waterfall, but there is nothing relating in the same way to dogs.

So we have a phrase that I believe we've all used at times, yet it seems so totally weird. I know of instances where fish and frogs have been swept into the air and raining down - that seems so much more believable. But cats and dogs – I don't think so.

Are You a Big Fish in a Small Sea or a Small Fish in a Big Sea
by Peter Debnam

You firstly need to ask yourself at what point in your life have you reached. Are you very important in the social group to which you primarily belong or have special well developed skills or talent lacking in others around you. If you do (or think you do) does that please you and give you a sense of contentment and pleasure? Or are you frustrated and feel it is time to move on and join a bigger social group where you feel you have more to offer? You need to consider why you want to move on- is it genuine frustration, ambition perhaps or is there some arrogance in your thinking? By asking these questions you may discover something about you that you have never really thought about.

 You may not even realise you are a big fish in a small sea, which doesn't hit you until you jump or accept an offer you simply can't refuse! Better to be prepared than suddenly find yourself in a big sea, where very quickly you realise you are a minnow surrounded by many people around you much more skilled and talented than yourself, or even worse, highly competitive Sharks!

There is a lot to be said for remaining in a small sea. We often hear about people whose work life has been mundane and repetitive yet shine in their social world in whatever genre they enjoy as leaders i.e. a big fish. This is not always the case and a striking example of this is the EU Referendum. The UK is a relatively small fish in a big sea, ruled by unelected politicians from more than 20 nations which we were uncomfortable with. So the Brexiteers won the day and now we are a big fish in a smaller sea. Or are we? Has our sense of self-importance left us as a much smaller fish in an enormous ocean full of sharks! Do your daffodil producers and even our fishermen now think we are a big fish in a small sea – I think not! I have quoted this example to show the complexities and ambiguities of our cliché i.e. small fish or big fish, is the grass truly greener on the other side or be careful what you wish for!!!

In 1633 the known world believed the Earth was the centre of the Heavens with the Sun and all the stars rotating around us ie: a big fish. It was Galileo who informed us of the error of current thinking at the time, explaining that it was the Sun at the centre (the big fish) and that Earth was merely revolving around it (the small fish). His thinking all but cost him is life as the Catholic Church exiled him to house arrest. Yet only two weeks ago we learnt that there are trillions of star systems in the Universe, leaving Earth as one of the tiniest fish in an enormous sea. Perhaps we would do well to stay that way and be less keen to go where no man has been before!!

Exercise - Write Something About Love

Finding the Word
by Michael Dudley

Shortly after I retired, I had a life changing experience and learned how to express my sensations of love.

I had been able to arrange an extended visit to the western lands of the USA. I had also managed to purchase a caravan and truck in which to travel and live for the next two years.

I achieved my goal to travel in the Western USA from the east (the Mississippi river) to the north (the glacier mountains on the Canada/ Montana border), from the west coast Pacific shores to the south (the border between Mexico and California) and back again.

Starting on my journey, which was now more like a pilgrimage, I was singing the country and western song 'On the Road Again' which quickly became my journey's theme song.

I also realised that when writing my journal, I needed new words to describe what I was experiencing and feeling. My problem was that the absolute wonder, the beauty of the nature I was passing through needed too many words, most of which I did not have. Then, one day, I had the feeling of love float over me; love not only for the nature I was immersed in at every turn, but for the journey itself – I was feeling love for what I was experiencing. And then came the word "WOW!!!" expressing exactly what I was feeling – the love for what I was doing – all the time.

WOW is a sixteenth century Scottish word but only now had it come to me for my special use throughout my travels.

It has become the expression of my experience of life which I was able to use in so many different ways during my travels and subsequently at any time, even now!

Have you ever been WOW'd?

Love Poems
by Brenda Heale

Cupid

Love Poem 1

I'm with somebody new

but I think of you

dressed in the latest fashion.

We were sweet 16

the teenage dream

and boy, I miss the passion!

Love Poem 2

When I was young and everything sweet

the places I'd go to

the people I'd meet

the things I would do

the ambition

the hope.

But then falling in love

oh, that slippery slope…

then it's marriage and babies

and mortgage and bills

non-stop arguments

and anti-depressant pills.

So the only advice

I can give from this rhyme

is don't fall in love

just have a bloody good time!

Love
by Peter Debnam

Do you really understand that Love or desire drives everything we do? Ask a psychiatrist and they will confirm it. Don't believe me? Well look at yourself right now and you will find that you are feeling a desire of one sort or another – annoyance, anger or perhaps that I am talking a lot of nonsense. Even when people say 'I don't get emotional', they are in fact already expressing a feeling, reflecting what their rational mind has stored up through their life experiences.

Our brain has two parts, the rational, thinking part and the emotional feeling part. Medical Science tells us that feelings begin in the womb between 24 and 28 weeks, and that new born babies can only initially express feelings. But as they grow and learn, their developing rational mind, largely based on what they find is pleasurable, expresses itself through feelings of either love or hatred or the myriad of feelings between these two extremes.

A recent example of this would be the scientists who used their great intellects to find a COVID vaccine, but they were driven by the desire or love to save mankind.

The problem is, what is love for one person or groups of persons is hatred for another, or is it?

An easy example is that half the voters in the USA love Donald Trump, but the other half hate him! Those who love him is because the life they have had and loved harmonises with his position. But the other half of the population hate him because Donald represents everything that works against their personal beliefs and values. But here's the big question! Are not both sides actually reflecting love of their position!? If it is, it proves the great religious tenet that good will always and inevitably triumph over evil.

Food for thought, eh?

Love Transformed
by Peter Duxbury

Roman sacrifice of goats

rewritten for a saint,

for to be a saint

you must a martyr be,

like Valentines to lose their heads,

from handmaid's tale,

rewritten for lovebirds

of Chaucer and Shakespeare,

now become chocolate, rose and card,

rewritten with hope for love

on one day a year.

Maybe one type of hopeless love

Valentine to seek attention.

For the eighth type of love seeks no attention,

no-self

lies in the source of spirit,

spirit in world soul.

Lilith, Adam, Panagia

in balance know the power,

yin flows yang

masculine in feminine, feminine in masculine

prism of eighty genders

spectrum's divergent attraction

birth's alignment of golden thread.

Align our paths on Earth

with the earth

green shoots

with roots so deep

intertwined in movement

in and out of passionate embrace,

fluid as amorphous amoeba

to love and be loved

with absence of separation......is all.

Eight Types of Love

Panagia – Our Earth, Life, Mother

Love
by Sheila Winckles

Jenny and Laura were on their way home from school. They lived a few doors from each other in the same road and over the years had become the greatest of friends.

They had no secrets from each other and discussed any problems they might have, knowing each could be trusted not to betray their secrets.

"Jenny, what did you think of Miss Baker's scripture lesson about St. Valentine and the way they put him to death in the 12th century? I thought it was really gruesome especially when his name is associated with love!" said Laura pulling a face.

"I know what you mean. Isn't it Valentine's Day next week? I know my sister is moping about and hoping that boy Derek in the next road will send her a card."

"I think my brother must have a sweetheart too because I noticed he had an envelope in his hand the other day and I've never known him to post a letter to anyone. When I mentioned it to mum she smiled and put her fingers to her lips and said it was none of our business and we mustn't say anything or laugh at Brian." Then she said "You never know, you might receive one from an admirer!"

Jenny looked at her friend and they both had a fit of the giggles.

"Well here we are home again, home again! And who knows how many admirers have written to us today!"

And with that they blew a kiss to each other and went into their own homes.

The Love is There
by Ann Weatherall

They say there's so much love around,

I know some don't believe it.

I wasn't sure myself at first, I thought it was all lies.

Then one day when I felt so low, and I needed someone near,

all my friends were far too busy to lend a listening ear.

So I sat right down and asked for help to see me through the days,

and to take all my heavy burdens far, far away.

It was on a Sunday morning that I walked into the church,

I sat right at the back, not wanting to disturb.

And when the service was over, two people came to me,

then three and four and several more

all shaking hands and hugging me.

The love I felt was such a thrill, so big and strong and bright.

I wanted this forever and I wouldn't lose the fight.

I suddenly found I had more friends, who loved me just for me,

They showed me love was everywhere, and truly it was free!

They showed me that I wasn't alone, and that all I had to do,

was reach out and connect through prayer, and love would follow through.

So now I know that love exists, and I'll never be alone.

Like a golden halo around me shining like the moon.

So when I'm feeling down, unloved and in a mess,

I'll remember that my life is filled with love and happiness.

Romance
by Arnold Sharpe

Should I attempt to write a love story, a romance, a tale of unrequited love? A tale of jealousy, revenge and yes, hatred. A tale of heroes, heroines, villains, and temptresses.

Let's see.

Mankind has nothing to thank that arch-temptress Eve for. In the Garden of Eden, she persuaded Adam to taste the apple from the tree of life. I hope it had a delicious taste because that action has caused nothing but mayhem ever since.

Let's face it, from the beginning of time love has been the root cause of wars, duels, murder, kidnapping etc. etc. Just think of Helen of Troy for starters. But then again if it hadn't been for her abduction Homer would have had little to write about.

Another chap who needs a closer look at is Valentine. This gentleman was a Roman who lived nearly two thousand years ago, seventeen hundred years ago to be more precise. Since his canonisation, he has been associated with courtly love. This must be where the term courtship came from. St. Valentine is also the Patron Saint of beekeepers and therein lies the sting.

Over the centuries authors and poets have had a field day when writing about love and romance. In real life, over the same period, countless men and women have been driven to distraction because of the allure and attraction of the opposite sex.

Coming to more modern times the power of 'sexism' is now making ground. No longer does a chap visit the local Pally in search of romance. No longer does a woman drop a handkerchief or use some other device to attract attention. The modern way to find a companion is to sit in front of a laptop and type in your details then try to find a match. For this, you pay a fee. (A thought here). Since when is one completely honest about one's personal details?

Modern children are now guarded against the insidious and hidden meanings within traditional fairy stories. Handsome princes and damsels in distress are now considered sexist, and feminist. Their stories can lead to sleepless nights among some young children. Even worse, when the heroine is put to sleep for a hundred years by an evil witch casting an evil spell, it gives the wrong impression for a male person to come and wake her up with a kiss without her permission. What is that charming prince to do? He can't kiss her without permission, but can he leave her to sleep her life away? No more princes or damsels in distress. Equal rights for all and let sleeping beauties remain asleep.

Using the terms he and she are no longer thought to be proper. A person is a person is a person and should only be categorised by one of the thousand and one classifications of gender. Old-fashioned courtship is now frowned upon.

Males need to be careful because this may make them susceptible to claims of historical sexual harassment later in life. Possibly by sending a bunch of flowers or, (don't tell Valentine), by sending one of his cards without permission. Males are now often abused for offering a seat to a lady on a busy bus or train.

Romance is not dead but in our modern times, it is becoming very different. In the good old days of romantic films the hero and heroine would, after many misunderstandings, fall into each other's arms, kiss and the camera would then pan away. Shall we say the modern version leaves little to the imagination?

I have used the terms he and she, male and lady. For those whom I have offended, I apologise.

Am I a romantic? Can I be a romantic? Yes I can and yes I am, but I'm also a cynic. Should I write a love story? Am I even capable of writing a romantic story?

Perhaps not.

Love Darts
by Maria Kinnersley

Psyche jumped as the door banged open. Her beloved husband stomped into the room. Throwing his quiver of arrows and bow into a corner, she dodged as red and black stars shot everywhere.

Cupid flung himself into a chair and sat at the table with his hands supporting his chin; his bow-shaped lips forming a pout and his golden curls shaking. It took no prize for Psyche to guess that her husband had not had a good day.

"How goes it, loved one?" she said in honeyed tones.

He stared at her.

"What's up?"

"What's up?" he roared. "I'll tell you what's up," he continued, his fingers making commas in the air. "I'm no longer needed in this world. I go out and about and no one wants to know. They wander around with their eyes on their mobiles, with no thought to love."

He buried his head in his hands and his shoulders shook. As he looked back at his wife, she was shocked to see tears streaking his cheeks. Something must be done, she thought.

Going to a wide bowl on a stand by the window, she gazed at the liquid within. Yes, she noted sadly, it was as he said. Then, she looked again.

"Husband," she said. "Look here."

He hauled himself from the seat, dragging his feet as he approached her.

"Well?" he responded with a gloomy tone.

"Observe that town, over there," she said pointing to the side nearest the window. "That's Bovey Tracey." Then she indicated excitedly, "I think that building is called Phoenix Hall. And look!!" she continued, "there are no mobiles. They're chatting together as they go into the hall."

He stared at the vision, then at her. "But they're…"

She glared at him. "Cupid, you ageist pig. What makes you think that you have to be young to fall in love? I challenge you," she continued, "Do your work there so you will have something to show for it on St Valentine's Day."

The following day, the door burst open. At the threshold, Cupid stood with a big smile on his face. His bow was in his hand and the arrows in the quiver over his shoulder bubbled pink hearts.

Psyche grinned. "I can see you've had a good day."

"Wonderful," he roared. That bunch at Phoenix Hall are marvellous. You never know," he continued with a wink, "My arrows may just have hit their mark."

What Matters?
by Maria Kinnersley

The doorbell rang, once, twice, three times.

"Okay, okay. Cut it out, I'm coming!" Ann yelled.

She lumbered to the door, her slippers only just about staying on her feet, and fumbled with the lock to open the door.

"What's all the row about Susie?" she asked the figure stood on the doorstep.

"Oh, Ann," the woman gasped. "You're my best friend and I wanted to tell you what my sister has been up to...again!" She grimaced.

"I thought you two were getting on better," Ann said as she led the way into the kitchen. She grabbed the kettle and gestured. Susie nodded.

Without waiting for the tea to be made, her visitor began.

"She's up to her old tricks again," she blurted. "I told her I wanted nothing more to do with her, that she'll be out of my life for good."

Ann remained silent while she bustled around, opening a biscuit tin and pouring boiling water into each tea-bagged mug. When all was ready, she sat at the table and patted the seat beside her. Susie slumped down, her face set in a frown which marred her handsome features.

"Susie, love," Ann began. "You must have known when you two found each other again that you wouldn't get on all the time. Families don't." She reached forward and patted her friend's hand. "Go back and make up. Families are what matters. You'll regret it if you don't."

Susie gave a reluctant nod of her head. She took a sip of the hot tea. As she replaced it on the table, her eyes widened. She jerked to her feet and grabbed her bag.

"I must go," she whispered. Her face had gone white. "Before she..."

With that, she fled the house, slamming the door behind her.

"Oh dear," Ann murmured, picking up her own mug. "What have you done now?"

What Matters
by Maria Kinnersley

Love is what matters,

Love is the key.

Without love, there is nothing

That matters more to me.

The world that we live in,

The people we meet,

Our friends and our family,

They matter to me.

Love for our planet,

Its resources and beauty,

To remember our care for it

As a loving duty.

Love for mankind,

Regardless of colour or creed.

And to be the help that is necessary

In times of great need.

Love for our families,

Though different they may be.

Love is the answer

When disturbance we see.

Love for ourselves,

Remember, we too matter.

To care for ourselves

Then love we can scatter

Tree Trail
by Doug Dunn

We gathered this month
in Mill Marsh Park for a
tree trail activity lunch.

It was once a field of cattle
marshland given to our town
Now trees are all around.

We heard that alder
have male and female flowers
hanging out together.

Next we found acorns
flat and pointed on their tops
of pin oak they were born.

Then on to Oregon
by a huge red trunk we stood

of a tall coast redwood.

Next was one we knew

from its silver pealing bark.

T'was the leaning silver birch.

Then not so well-known

We stood by a pear-shaped tree.

The hard green hornbeam.

After a rain shower

we picked apples then found

sweet chestnuts on the ground.

On the avenue

were leaves with dunces hats!

Tiny lime tree mites.

Last we saw a maple tree.

Bright leaves around and

From its boughs

Mistletoe hung down.

We thanked the Reverend Michael

joining Chris and Colin's band

then we all thanked Daphnie and

Bovey Tracey's pleasant land.

Norway Maple Tree

Fun Exercise - Use the following 25 words in a 500-word story:

drag anchor; radio; gaiety; shortage; hollow; UFO; instruction; flamingo; marble; jargon; pipe; knuckle;

temple; bury; anorak; eagle; wicket; petty; youth; quarter; churn; shuffle; lobster; naughty; ogre

The Final Match of the Season
by Arnold Sharpe

The final match of the season. The winners to be crowned League Champions.

Chasing 207 runs to win, Bovey had had the upper hand until a disastrous collapse. Seventeen runs still required. John Temple 107 not out facing the Chudleigh attack. A further eleven runs scored when calamity struck again. Howzat? John given out LBW first ball of the final over spotted by the *eagle*-eyed umpire.

James, last man in had to *shuffle* across his crease and duck to avoid the bouncer that had been hurled at him by, reputedly, the leagues fastest bowler. To lose another *wicket* would mean defeat. At six feet tall and well-built, James was no shrinking violet, but this bowler was doing his best to intimidate him. To tell the truth, James thought, he was succeeding. The bowler gave James one of those smiles that said he was enjoying himself. *Petty* James thought.

Four more balls to face, six runs required. Watching Alex slowly retreat to the end of his run up, James wondered if a dose of Covid might be more preferable. The morning's news on the *radio* had featured that formidable duo Professor Guess, an expert in worse case scenarios and Professor Fear, who had said Covid could last for years.

James was brought suddenly back to the present as he saw Alex reaching the end of his run up. James's stomach began to *churn*, the *hollow* feeling then replaced by a *shortage* of breath. This *ogre* of a baller started his charge. No *quarter* given. He remembered the *instruction* he'd been given; *knuckle* down and concentrate.

The next ball was, however, somewhat slower and allowed James to *drag* the ball to leg side and *bury* it to the boundary. A feeling of euphoria overwhelmed James.

The fourth and fifth balls of the over both stuck James in the body, joy for the bowler, pain for the batsman and two runs still needed. *Anchor* one end he had been told, *pipe* dreams he mused. They say *youth* has no fears. How, James wished that was true.

Alex was now preparing to ball the last ball of the innings. Two runs needed. James thoughts however drifted back to Covid. Why should some *anorak* in his *marble* hall spew out so much *jargon* and prophesise a *temple* of doom?

Tonight, he had arranged to meet his mates at the *Naughty Lobster* the best night club in town, they charged exorbitant prices, but so what.

Concentrate, Alex was on his way. He would put everything into this final ball of the match. The ball flew at him like a *UFO*. He ducked, his bat dangling by his side. The ball caught the edge of his bat lobbing over the wicket keeper's head. James sprinted the first run; the fielder fumbled the ball. The race was on for the winning run, fame was within his grasp. Out of nowhere a giant *flamingo* landed and stopped his onrush.

All *gaiety* ceased. James sat bolt upright in bed. His morning alarm screaming in his ears.

Visitation
by Rosie Curling

Slipping on my anorak, I quickly left the party as all fun and gaiety had abruptly ceased after a radio announcement that a UFO had landed two miles away on Lobster Beach.

I ran through the gardens of the old castle, past the ancient hollow oak, past the temple with the strange marble flamingo on one side of the entrance, and an eagle on the other, apparently part of the family crest, steeped in the mysteries of time.

I am a journalist, and in these strange times much space activity is being reported with many sightings of space-ships landing up and down the country - my instructions were to get there quickly, tell it as it is, using as little scientific jargon as possible - people were getting excited, hopeful and intrigued by the frequent arrivals, and the soothing light and haunting music that accompanied them, prompted rumours that the occupants were benign entities with great healing powers - many people felt increased well-being after being bathed in the light surrounding the ships. Rumours abounded that they had heard of our anguish and fear from their home in the universe and had come to help us.

Our emotions churned between hope and despair as we sought to bury our negative feelings, and reach out to our salvation; the youth of our country were unanimous, their faith unshakeable, these beings were our hope and salvation, no petty doubts clogged their young minds and hearts.

I reached the edge of the beach and felt peace flood over me as I listened to the music. I shuffled slowly from shadow to shadow trying to remain invisible, until I was less than a quarter of a mile away. A crowd had gathered quietly absorbing the healing light flooding over them. The door of the ship opened. A majestic, powerful but extremely gentle Being stood there framed in the archway. The light blazed covering all who stood there - total peace descended as we felt a new strength flow through us and glimpsed a new way of living.

I ran, stumbling over the pebbles in my haste to tell of this amazing experience. I fell twice grazing my knuckles, breaking my treasured pipe (my companion since university). Nothing mattered anymore, neither loss nor pain had any significance. A shining new path lay ahead for us all for the Ogre Covid 19 was defeated.

Printed in Great Britain
by Amazon

27749887R00119